Listen for a Whisper

Listen for a Whisper

Prayers,
Poems,
and
Reflections
by
Girls

Edited by Janet Claussen
and Marilyn Kielbasa

Saint Mary's Press • Christian Brothers Publications • Winona, Minnesota

Genuine recycled paper with 10% post-consumer waste.
Printed with soy-based ink.

The publishing team included Marilyn Kielbasa and Janet Claussen, development editors; Gabrielle Koenig, copy editor and production editor; Amy Schlumpf Manion, typesetter; Cären Yang, designer; manufactured by the production services department of Saint Mary's Press.

Jennifer Riska, cover artist, Winona Voices Group, Winona, MN.

Printed in the United States of America

Printing: 9 8 7 6 5 4 3 2

Year: 2009 08 07 06 05 04 03 02

ISBN 0-88489-685-4

Library of Congress Cataloging-in-Publication Data

Listen for a whisper : prayers, poems, and reflections by girls / edited by Janet Claussen and Marilyn Kielbasa.
    p. cm.
    Summary: More than two hundred prayers, poems, and reflections on faith,
hope, love, and God, by girls ages eleven to eighteen, selected from Catholic schools and parishes throughout the country.
    ISBN 0-88489-685-4 (pbk.)
    1. Teenage girls—Prayer-books and devotions—English. 2. Catholic Church—Prayer-books and devotions—English. [1. Prayer books and devotions. 2. Children's writings. 3. Youths' writings.] I. Kielbasa, Marilyn. II. Claussen, Janet.
BX2150 .L49 2001
242'.633—dc21
                                                                    2001002443

Contents

Preface

In June 1998, Saint Mary's Press hosted the first meeting of what was to become the steering committee for the Voices Project, an initiative of Saint Mary's Press to nurture and support the spiritual life of girls and young women. The group consisted of five women who were actively involved in the life of girls as teachers, youth ministers, community organizers, and counselors. The premise of the Voices Project is that girls and boys approach spirituality differently. Each gender brings different experiences, inherent traits, cultural norms, and societal expectations to their spiritual life.

One of the suggestions that came from the steering committee was to compile a book of poems, prayers, and reflections by girls as a way of listening to their voices and peeking into their souls. The book would also be a way for girls to share with one another the joys and struggles of being a girl today.

We sent out about six thousand invitations to schools and parishes across the country, inviting girls in the sixth to twelfth grades to send us their thoughts, using the following questions as guidelines:

- What is your experience of God?
- Who is God for you?
- How has God touched your life?
- What gives you hope and inspiration?
- From whom or from where have you learned most about God?
- Where do you see God?
- What and who is important in your life?

We received an overwhelming response to our invitation. About twelve hundred girls sent in prayers, poems, and reflections. The task that faced us was to choose about two hundred from among those submitted. It was a difficult job because each of the pieces came from the heart and mind of a girl who was hoping to see her work in the book. In the interest of space, paper, and balance in a variety of areas, we had to set aside many prayers, poems, and reflections that were well worthy of publication. If your piece or that of one of the girls you work with was not included in the book, it is not likely because the prayer was not good or that the reflection was not meaningful. We honestly wish we could have included them all.

Contained in this book are many different voices of girls as they make their way through life, guided by their Creator and the people who accompany them on their journey to wholeness and holiness. We hope that this book of prayers, poems, and reflections is one of many steps along our path to recognizing, hearing, validating, and celebrating the unique spiritual experiences of girls and young women.

Janet Claussen and Marilyn Kielbasa
Editors

Voices of faith,
hope,
and love

I spy with my little eye . . .
a child, God's baby doll.
I spy with my little eye . . .
a light, God's flashlight in the dark.
I spy with my little eye . . .
a bird, God's kite to fly on a sunny day.
I spy with my little eye . . .
a flower, a beauty in God's garden.
I spy with my little eye . . .
the sun, God's light into the room.
I spy with my little eye . . .
a star, God's eyes looking down on every one of us.
I spy with my little eye . . .
water, a puddle God jumps in on a rainy day.
I spy with my little eye . . .
a cloud, God's couch to lie on on the weekend.
I spy with my little eye . . .
the earth, God's dollhouse to play with.
I spy with my little eye . . .
me, God's own image.

Erin A. Frey, age 13
Saint Sabina School, Florissant, MO

I guess I figured it out last year at Fourth of July. I mean I really understood God's plan for us. First of all you have to know that I spend the Fourth at my Grandma Rita's house, and I have about thirty-two cousins on that side of the family. I am best friends with all of my cousins, but there is a special group that I like to hang out with when we get together. We were all together in one corner of the field that Fourth of July, waiting for the others to start shooting the fireworks. While we were all waiting for it to get dark, we started talking about everything and anything that came to mind. We rambled on for a while and then **WHOOSH! BOOM!** We hadn't noticed that they had lit the first rocket. We all "oohed" and "aahed" in appreciation and watched intently for about ten minutes. After that, however, we started to talk again because we have seen this kind of stuff as long as we can remember. For a while I talked to them without looking at them, watching the fireworks, but when Kara said something surprising I looked over at all of them. We continued to talk, this time I was turned and talking to their faces. I started to notice that when it was dark (and it was very dark by now), you could only see outlines, and it was just enough to know that they were still there. However, you could see every face and feature when the fireworks lit up the sky.

Now you might be really wondering how this relates to God. While I was daydreaming in church the next morning, I figured out what was happening. My cousins were like God (don't take me literally, use your imagination). Even when I couldn't see them all the way, I knew they were there. In fact, I was talking to them just like you might talk to God even when you're not sure God is there. The fireworks were what God wants us to be. When they exploded, they illuminated my cousins (or God). God wants us to show others what God is really like. To do this we need a spark, just like a lighter is to the rockets. This spark could be anything from an inspiring passage from the Bible to church leaders or our parents. We might have a long way to travel just to do something for someone else, whether that be in miles or through overcoming a fear, and that distance may be straight up. Who knows? When we get past those obstacles we are ready to explode. We need to be as big and as bright as we can when it comes to our God. We need to make the biggest impact we can. But most of all we need to illuminate God as brightly and as long as we can. Think about it, find your spark, overcome your obstacles, and shine long and bright and illuminate our God for everyone to see.

Jamie L. Adams, age 14
Saint James Parish, Liberty, MO

Have you ever felt so close to heaven and God that all you can do is cry—not out of sadness or loneliness, but out of pure and simple joy? I was blessed to experience this at a youth conference I attended. As a pastor was preaching, he would spontaneously break into simple but moving songs. One that he sang, along with everyone in the stadium, contained the words, "Answer Me!" I had been fighting many internal battles and had been preoccupied with several situations in my life, but the moment this little prayer was being sung to God, tears welled up in my eyes and an internal peace consumed my whole being. I felt the Lord's presence surround and settle within me. I was overwhelmed with the joy and grace that only can be received from Jesus. The comfort and relief that God's presence gave me was so entrancing. I stayed as still as I possibly could, not wanting this magnificent feeling to leave me. I could not say a word; I only could shed tears of joy!

Naomi Dudek, age 16
Saint Pius X Parish, Rochester, NY

Stormy Faith

I feel your rain of mercy on my shoulders.
I see your beam of healing within my soul.
I hear the boom of your strength surrounding my heart.
Yet I am weak, my eyes are blind, my ears are deaf.
But your storm of heaven continues still.
Why do I lay still?
Why do I shield my eyes?
Why do I cover my ears?
Lord, help me open up to your grace.
Let your rain soak in me, your beam amaze my eyes, and
   your boom strengthen me.
God clear me of storms and let the warmth of your Son
   soothe my spirit. Amen.

Ellen Wagner, age 13
Annunciation School, Webster Groves, MO

I watched the roaring fire,
Burning brightly in the night.
Mesmerizing colors,
Providing warmth and light.
Time to pray and ponder,
Before the embers die.
Dreams of burning wonder,
Reaching toward the sky.
Please help me to understand,
To walk with you and start.
To only see what really counts,
The power of my heart.
Holy Spirit, burn within,
Fill me with the light.
Spiritual fire help me,
Power, strength, and might.

Meghan Beardsley, age 16
Our Lady of Mercy Academy, Syosset, NY

How can I describe for you
With the language of humans
That which God has given?

How can I relate it to you
This Spirit of love
If you have not felt it?

It is the Spirit that is glorious
That enables you to love
That makes it all good.

How can I even paint the picture?
No color can depict it,
No human hand design it.

It is the Spirit that is shown
That only the heart can see
That the heart believes.

So don't hold yourself away,
Obey your heart.
Go to the Spirit.

The Spirit is strength.
The Spirit is love.
The Spirit is truth.

Julie R. Freyou, age 17
Saint Joseph Academy, Baton Rouge, LA

Religious Doubts

My experience with the Catholic religion is lifelong. Born into
a strong Catholic family, I neither knew of nor was exposed to
other faiths growing up. My religion wasn't my choice, and my
forced faith in God is a result of that. Now, I am in my eleventh

year of Catholic school, and as I start to really learn about Catholicism, I am starting to doubt my faith, even though I reaffirmed it in the sacrament of Confirmation recently. Part of me reasons that God and Jesus are just ideas that people believe in as a source of comfort. I am starting to read the Bible with logic, rather than trusting that it was God's power at work. Doubt is just a small part of me. The part of me that hopes my doubts aren't true prays every night in belief that there actually is a God listening to me.

K. T. Dixon, age 16
Regina High School, Harper Woods, MI

I'm falling away from the light in my soul, the love in my life, the truth in the world.
I'm reaching for illusions and ghostly apparitions. My fingers slip through these illusory things, and yet somehow I find them covered with blood.
I feel in my heart a throbbing reminder, a soothing rhythm of something hopeful and beautiful and spiritual.
The sleepy sound soothes me, gently moves me. I can feel it deep within. Somehow I suddenly see it so clearly, the light in my soul, the love in my life, the truth in the world.
No words, only tears, effortless smiles, joy from within.
I have found myself.
I uncovered my strength.
I am inspired.
I am hopeful.
I am flying, guided by the light in my soul, the love in my life, the truth in the world.

Stacey Ramsower, age 17
Salpointe Catholic High School, Tucson, AZ

Lord God,
You continually watch over our world;
Please help us to always strive for equality for all people.
Do not let people judge others by the color of their skin or their
    sex.
Help us to see through all of the differences,
Instead let us see what is in their hearts.
Help all people feel good about who they are,
Help everyone feel equality,
Not injustice.
Amen.

JoAnne M. Hrabovsky, age 14
Holy Spirit School, Pequannock, NJ

*I pray to the One who created me, and the One who will
    take me after my time on earth.*
I pray to the One who has lifted me, guided me, helped me, and
    loved me unconditionally.
I pray to the One to whom many are devoted, the One who has
    captured the love of many.
I pray to the One who has so much power, who doesn't use that
    power to conquer or to gain more power, but uses it to help
    people, for love of the people.
I pray to the One who created Jesus, our Savior, the perfect
    human.
I pray to the One who accepts all, loves all, and cares for all.
I pray to the One who is free of sin, and to the One I strive to be
    like more and more each day.
I pray to God.

Nancy T. Sprovieri, age 12
Saint Charles Borromeo Parish, Skillman, NJ

As I am walking down a row of almond trees,
I whisper, "God where are you? Do You see me?"
I turn around to see a sign due to me,
but instead I see nothing.
Only the humming of the bumblebees.
I repeat once more, "God, why don't you show your face to me,
    please?"
I look up to the heavens,
waiting for a bright light to blind my eyes.
But instead all I see is a white dove flying by.
Patiently, again I say, "Why must you be so aggravating, my dear
    God, I pray?"
I look at the almond tree,
waiting for a white rose to appear to me,
but all I see is a lonesome pink bud, budding in front of me.
Red-faced and angered, at last I say,
"God, I pray to you, and I believe in you.
But how can I believe in someone I do not see?"
I trip and fall on a stick I did not see,
and my eye catches on a beautiful, pastel-colored rainbow.
And finally it all hits me.
The bees, the bird, the pink bud, and the beautiful rainbow:
These are no regular things.
These are all happenings and gifts from God.
How could I have been so blind?
Every time I asked God to appear to me,
God did—just not in the form I expected it to be.
How grateful I am to God,
for all I have and for all the times God is there
for me and with me!

Mary Terese Galas, age 14
Saint Stanislaus School, Modesto, CA

Hiding in the dark
I sit alone,
cold and trembling in the gray mental haze.
The door cracks slightly open.
My eyes raise,
bloodshot and teary.
A small ray of light
projects on my hand.
I close my eyes again,
wishing for the pain to go away.
I hear the hinges creak,
more light . . .
more heat . . .
Who is here with me in the **dark?**
I shudder.
The cold seizes my body.
I yearn to be warm again,
to feel love. . . .
A silent breeze sweeps over me,
smelling of sweet aromatic flowers.
I am calm.
I feel you near.
I am not alone.
I never was.

Jennifer Aikens, age 16
Bishop Guilfoyle High School, Altoona, PA

Dear Wonder,
When I think about the Eucharist, it seems sort of odd that a
piece of wheat could mean so much. When I think of God's
body I think of more than a small piece of the simplest wheat,
but I guess it means more. Christ was one man out of many;
therefore the smallness of the Eucharist. Christ was also a simple

man, and so simple wheat. Christ is also part of all of us, and when we receive this Body of Christ, we receive Christ in a more human or realistic form. We come to understand Christ through accepting him in the form of the Eucharist. By giving us the Eucharist, Christ is allowing us to share in his life, and to grow with him. The Eucharist is God's presence in the world, and an invitation to join in this presence.

Julie Heidger, age 18
Saint Joseph Academy, Saint Louis, MO

Sometimes late at night I look
up at the heavens, at the shining stars.
And then I feel they were made just for us,
that every one is a gift from God.

For every flower in the world
is a treasure of endless worth.
So if I have a garden of flowers,
I have a trove of treasures indeed.

For every memory I have of a friend,
there is a story of friendship to tell.
And every time I hear someone laugh
it's a reminder of reasons to smile.

So now I claim with happiness
that I've been blessed,
that I've been given what I value most
and treasure above the rest.

I have felt love, I have known peace.

And so I thank God down on my knees.
Thank you for Life—this precious gift.

Graciela Cristina Carrasco, age 13
Academia María Reina, San Juan, PR

Dear God,
You have given me everything, yet I have nothing to give you in
   return.
How can I, a mere human, repay you, Creator of heaven and
   earth?
I may be young, but this I understand: you have given me all that
   I have—my life, my family, my talents, my dreams.
Only one thing I can hope is that you will accept all my love.
Amen.

Clare Wrobel, age 12
Saint Joseph School, Lake Orion, MI

Goddition

Death + God = Life
Mean + God = Kind
Frown + God = Smile
Winter + God = Spring
Helpless + God = Independent
Weak + God = Power
Ignorance + God = Knowledge
Decrease + God = Increase
Fruitless + God = Bearing
Enemy + God = Friend
Hate + God = Love
Cold + God = Warm
Captivity + God = Freedom
War + God = Peace
Jealous + God = Content
Sad + God = Happy

Kirsten Johnson, age 12
Saint Pius X, Edgewood, KY

God gives me hope and inspiration. When I'm tired, or when I want to quit something, God is always there to cheer me on. I hear God's soft and gentle voice in my heart saying, "Don't give up!" God's words give me encouragement, and make me feel more confident. I think that even though I don't hear God's voice cheering me on, that if I believe, God will always cheer me on from my heart.

Grace Cho, age 11
Our Lady Help of Christians School, Los Angeles, CA

Are you there God,
How can I tell?
What do you see
When you look at me?
Do you see my hopes and dreams,
Or my accomplishments ripped at the seams?
How can I be sure, God, that you are there,
When I have such a burden to bear?
Maybe it's that you don't have time,
To listen to me whine.
I know you are there God,
I can just tell.
But I still don't know what you see,
When you look deep into me.
I'm sure you look at my hopes and dreams,
And not my accomplishments that are slightly ripped
at the seams.
I am always sure that you are there,
Because you help me carry that burden I bear.
Maybe it's because you love and cherish me,
That you let me be who I want to be.

Molly Medina, age 15
Salpointe High School, Tucson, AZ

Faith
is something
that doesn't come in a
package. Faith is more like
a mountain. In order to be close
to God we have to climb the hill of
life. On that road are many things to slow
us down, rocks and roads that lead us astray
from the true course. Like temptation and sin.
Jesus had to climb that **MOUNTAIN** too. It's not hard
to slip or fall along the way, many of us have. There
have been times when I have slipped, or have just stopped along the way to think, but in the end, I will always
get back up again and start walking toward God. I climb
without fear because I know if I ever fall Jesus will be right
behind me, waiting to catch me, for he too knows how it
feels to fall. He too knows of the struggle to get close to God.
He knows how hard it is to resist temptation. He knows. He
too has been on the mountain with us. Lord, please help me on
my way to you. Encourage my growth and development. Listen
to me and answer my prayers. Catch me when I fall. Amen.

Katie McGroarty, age 13
Saint Odilia School, Shoreview, MN

I don't know if I really believe in God. I do pray to God all
the time. (The funny thing is eight out of ten times what I pray for
comes true!) I think we, as Catholics, want to believe in something so bad that we create a figure that we can look up to. I
think we are so afraid to die, we want to know that we're going
somewhere, so we don't think we turn into nothingness. At least,
that's how I feel. I want to believe so bad that we're going to go
somewhere. I still have problems believing in God. They say that
God loves us so much and forgives us. Then can you please

explain why God punished Adam and Eve so harshly? If God loved them and forgave them, they'd probably have lived in the garden their whole life. And another thing, if God forgives people, then are all those people in jail going to go to heaven? Does that mean there is no hell and that when we go to heaven there will be ax murderers up there with us?

I hope that there is a God. That way we'll not have wasted our life believing in something that's not even real.

Nicole K. Smith, age 11
Saint Joseph School, West Milford, NJ

Looking through my life, I've realized

You've been there for me when I have cried.

I called out your name, you answered my plea.
I probably didn't deserve it, but you didn't flee.

I never liked church and rarely ever prayed
Though at my side is where you stayed.

When I was in need, the only time I'd ask
I'd pray for you to help me, but that was the past.

I've figured it out, I need you so much—
Your guidance, your love, your spiritual touch.

I love you, God, what else can I say?
I need you tomorrow, I need you today.

Thank you for all that you've given me,
I was blind before, but now I can see.

I see you're the only thing true in my life.
You have helped me through the pain and the strife.

Katie Klein, age 14
Saint Pius X, Edgewood, KY

Be Still and Know That I Am God

Be with me as I walk, for we journey together. Hold my hand so my feet will stay on your path.

Still the noises around me so I can hear your voice; herald your angels' song so I can feel their sweet breath.

And know, Most High, that my feet are moving, my soul is listening, your spirit winds are in my fields and upon my face. That I might glorify your name spoken upon my heart, washed in the waters of your love, forever in your care.
I tremble before you, knowing you know who I am, seeking the forgiveness that only you, Most High, can grant my love.

Am I worthy to stand in your presence? To receive your greatest gift—Jesus. One word and I shall be healed.

Heavenly God, I beseech you to weave a fabric of your love, surround this single thread with joy.

Let it be your cloth upon which the banquet is spread.

Lesley Gilhooly, age 11
Saint Anne School, Houston, TX

You may not know love, but love knows you.

That is why everyone is born with love, but must be taught to hate.
Love is patient with you, so you must be patient with love.
Love and trust go hand in hand; so when you lose trust, you
    question love.
It's your choice, you love or you hate, but remember loving is the
    key to life, not hating.

Erin Elizabeth McMahon, age 12
Saint Joseph School, West Milford, NJ

Infamous Fate

Burn.
One Man BLAZES as intense iron
Penetrates two palms.
Dirt devours holy-washed feet.
Thorns of agony scorch One scalp.
Splinter-stricken ears cannot help but
Heed to the wailing,
Moaning of those who are embraced in this
Force of Infamous Fate.
His Holy Father illuminates the scene with flames of
Fiery heat.
Sweat cries,
Tears bleed as
Sadism exiles all peace, rendering rancor and roar.
One blistering body breathes for life
As One Demise delivers salvation for humanity.

Mary Beth Sales, age 15
Villa Duchesne Oak Hill School, Saint Louis, MO

I know that no matter what happens today

there is nothing I can't handle.
I know that I will not go
through anything alone.
I know that God is going to be there,
to give me strength and courage to do what I have to.
Knowing that gives me hope
and inspiration.

Megan Salvano
Sacred Heart Parish, Bangor, MI

I made a pledge
Some time ago
To be a servant of God.
To use the talents
That God has blessed me with
To go and help someone.
I signed this pledge
Without a thought of what it really meant.
"I'll go and help people
And smile a lot
And do whatever I can."
Looking back, I realize now
That my pledge to be a friend
Did not end with only a smile
Or a simple lend of hand.
Instead my pledge included
God and all the world,
To bring unity to the torn
smiles to the sad
And dignity to those whom have none.
For it is in Christ's body
Which we receive every Sunday
That we witness God's deepest calling:
To be brothers and sisters to the entire human race
And create the greatest community we can.

Rebecca Morrison, age 16
Assumption High School, Louisville, KY

All through the frenzied and frantic day,
Nothing seems to go right,
Friends are mad.
Forgot the homework.
Failed a test.
Waiting for the day to finally be over.
Then at home
Peace and quiet, praying
Brings a calm to the day
That nothing else in the world can bring.
Nothing chaotic, only tranquility,
A new level of being,
A personal, one-on-one relationship
With God.

Amanda Flato, age 14
Saint Agnes Academy, Houston, TX

Divine Peace

I feel the world is closing in on me,
Everything seems dark and stormy, but
there is one thing I can count on.

Whenever I'm in doubt,
Whenever I feel lonely,
Whenever I need inspiration,
There is one thing I can count on.

Suddenly one person comes into my mind,
I feel as calm as a summer's breeze,
Nothing can disturb my peace,
I feel love all around me.
I feel God.

Jennifer Prats-Díaz, age 18
Academia María Reina, San Juan, PR

Where is this God to whom I pray?
The faceless presence
Who fills gaps nothing else can.
Surely he is not in the breeze,
Which cools the body for a second
Then leaves you wanting more.
Surely she is not in what we say,
For no god could be so cruel so consistently.
Surely God could not be in our belongings—
Belongings we adore for a short time,
Complain about when they no longer are as shiny,
And then discard for the newer model.
So where is this Being we implore?
God is anywhere there is beauty and ugliness.
God is everywhere and everything.
We can never escape God's eyes,
His voice,
Her arms.
God is found where good can be created,
Wherever love is experienced,
Wherever we make mistakes.
This is where I see God,
And where God will always be.

T. R., age 17
Mercy Academy, Louisville, KY

My Calling

I yearned to see heaven,
And God showed it to me.
I yearned to feel love,
And God gave it to me,
I yearned to be cared for,
And God cared for me.
I yearned for compassion,
And God gave it to me.
I yearned for forgiveness,
And God forgave me.
I yearned to know what God wanted of me,
And God said,
  Go likewise and do for others
  what I have done for you.

Amanda Maisonneuve, age 16
Regina High School, Harper Woods, MI

I breathe in the Spirit
    let the soul go far beyond me
breeze of day
breath of life
       so inspiring
       so enlivening
we all are planted as trees
       to grow in the One we have come from
I grow, I sway
    sweet wind each day
and light to warm
       self that I am
       self that I was
                  become
    and return with my God to the land
all home
       and shadows of selves I believe
we flow
       like the grass in the field
       as the wild rushes over
turning each stem
blessing each root
       and connecting and guiding and coming and giving
such love such presence
all showers of dew
       and life reaches far beyond me
    like the branches of a tree
       stretching into the night sky
the prayer of a child whose heart is help,
    cradled by One who just is loving guiding knowing
       who just is
           echoes swirled around desert sands
natural faith
       soul's bond unbroken.

Lauren Michaela, age 17
Little Flower High School, Philadelphia, PA

The Answer

I find myself so often staring,
Staring into vastness and wondering,
Why did God let that happen?
Never understanding and always confused,
My life, spinning out of control.
There are too many questions
And not enough answers.
There is too much to know,
But not enough to learn.
I find myself falling and being trapped,
Feeling confused and frustrated and
Angered because life is not perfect.
But every now and then
I find myself staring and thinking
Maybe this is what God wants to happen.
Maybe this is perfect.
And maybe God wants to shine through me
And have me be the light for others.
"Speak, Lord, for your servant is listening."
(1 Samuel 3:9).

Katherine Tymchuck, age 14
Benilde-Saint Margaret Junior High, Saint Louis Park, MN

In the credulous eyes of a child
in a mother's hands,
in the fragrance of a blooming rose mild,
I find God.

In the eloquent intimidation of the ocean,
in the rise of the sun so fair,
in the graceful dancer's motion,
I find God.

And I see all this beauty surrounding me
And I wish to consume it all.
But I know it is in heaven
Where I will know God.

In the faintly whistling breeze,
in the power of love,
in those as luckless as autumn leaves,
I find God.

In the armored warrior's tears,
in the art of music's harmony,
in peaceful rest without fear,
I find God.

And I see all this magnificence surrounding me
And I wish to consume it all.
But I know that it is in heaven
Where I will be with God.

Andrea M. Suazo, age 17
Fort Worth, TX

Spirituality is the vision in my soul.
I take a path which I must follow,
to lead a life without pain and sorrow.
Each day brings me new choices,
I lead my life after the One who saved us.
I will live a new life with someone who cares.
When I reach the sky I will be there.
Spirituality is the vision in my soul.
I take a path that I must follow
to lead a life without pain and sorrow.

Megan Sheila Brennan, age 12
Sacred Heart Academy, Redlands, CA

I hope to show love
In all I say and do
And shine like God's sun
Bringing comfort to someone.

I hope to be kind and helpful
And very delightful
To be the best I can be
As God intended for me.

Alison Marie Heydle, age 12
Saint Luke School, Boardman, OH

God's Colorless Love

They say love is blind.
They say love has no color,
And I believe that.
But why do we live in
Black and white?
Why is color an issue?
If one can see so clearly,
Why can't another?
How can there be change,
In a world of prejudice.

When you find love,
You find it in the heart,
Not in the skin.
I believe in soul mates.
But how can one
Find their mate
If they only look halfway?
In the end,
We are all the same.
God created us all to love,
One another.
Not just one of our color.

So we must love all
And look beyond the apparent,
Search for the heart.
That heart which beats
Inside you and me.
It's playing God's music
For all to hear.
We just need to tune in.

Tiffany Smith, age 16
Towson Catholic High School, Towson, MD

I have an aging, cantankerous black cat, who has taught me a few lessons about life. There are several things he absolutely requires: Fancy Feast, someone to hold the door open, a warm lap. Only when his needs are met, and he is curled up in a purring ball, does he makes it clear to everyone that God is indeed on God's throne and all is right in the world.

I've decided that sometimes, maybe the less one actually peruses with knowledge and reasoning, the easier it is to understand. As human beings, we are not easily satisfied. There are many things I would like to know, but can't right now. It is a relief to stop fighting with questions. God, please let us have the faith of a contented cat. Help us to accept you without having to know why, and live curled up in your warm, holy lap.

Meredith Gilliam, age 15
Church of the Good Shepherd, Raleigh, NC

Faith is a kiss,
Not a peck-on-the-cheek,
Kiss-your-great-aunt-hello kiss,
But a pure, simple,
Passionate, radiant kiss.
It fills you with inane joy
That you could be part of
Something so wonderful!
Something so breathtaking!
It sweeps you off your feet
And makes even the depths
Of despair a cheery place to be.
This kiss is a piece of you,
Of who you are.
Sometimes the memory slips
To the back of your mind,
And you lose sight of the glory of it.
Yet when you really need it,
It comes pouring back,
To raise your self-esteem
To remind you that you are loved.
You can't say exactly what it is,
Merely that it's like being swept
Through a thunderstorm,
Yet in this turbulent zephyr,
You know no harm will come to you,
Faith is a kiss to the soul.

Brenna C. Gilbert , age 15
Academy of Notre Dame, Villanova, PA

God Is All Around Me

I feel God in the
sun
rain
wind
and
snow.
God is all around me.

I see God in the
clouds
stars
water
and
future.
God is all around me.

I hear God at
night
in my dreams
when I speak
and
when I think.
God is all around me.

No matter
where I am
when I am there
or
how I got there,
God will be with me every step of the way.

Jillian D'Amico, age 12
School of the Holy Child, Rye, NY

Breath of God
in the
soul of girls

God to me
is the wisdom
when I have
to choose
right from wrong.

God to me
is the courage
when I am
afraid
to face the world.

God to me
is the determination
when someone or something
stands in my way for
excellence.

God to me
is the light
when someone or everything
around me
appears to be in the dark.

God to me
is the wisdom,
the courage,
the determination,
and the light
of my life.

Sierra Latrice Scott, age 13
Sacred Heart Parish, Atlanta, GA

my mother
taught me little of God
just that God is
my father
she took me to the church
and i heard his many teachings
on cold sunday mornings
and sticky saturday afternoons
my schools
filled notebooks of
the parables preached
of God and his son
all about their love
and how God loves all
but in my mind
i felt this was not God
so i listened and i felt—
in the trees
in the grass
underneath the sun
the moon
the stars
i heard God's own words
and she has told me all i know
and now i know myself
and i know her.

Alison Keohane, age 16
Immaculate Heart Academy, Washington Township, NJ

I Saw You, God

I have seen you in other people.
I have seen little miracles.
I have seen you in words.
I have seen you in songs.
I have seen you in happy times.
I have seen you in bad times.
I have seen you in the crying baby.
I have seen you in the prison inmate.
I have seen you on the corner collecting.
I have seen you parched and dying.
I have seen you in the wandering man.
I have seen you all around,
. . . but I have just begun to see you in me.

Andrea Phillips, age 16
Saint Michael the Archangel Parish, Garland, TX

God is with me —in my thoughts and mind. I see God in my dreams. I talk to God every day. I think God is a human star, shining down on us like the sun. God gives me hope and inspiration. For me, God is a person who guides me when I'm in need. I value God and my family. The most important thing in life is my family.

Sarah Ceci, age 11
Saint Francis School, Ridgefield Park, NJ

God means love.
God means happiness.
God is everything.
God is almighty.
But to me God is
All of the above
And more.
God is my mother,
My sister, my father,
And everyone I care about.

N. L., age 12
A Place Called Home, Los Angeles, CA

A View of the Highest

Cares not only for one but all
Does not abandon in time of need
Instead stays and helps through
Is a guardian and protector
Sometimes, the phrase, "Why me?"
Rarely a definite answer
Faith, solution to possible despair
Sinners soon repent and plead
Source of calmness and forgiveness
A green tree, symbol of good and life
Rotting trunk, symbol of evil and death
Greatest contrasts share characteristics
Creator and divine power
God is the highest.

Isalice Acevedo, age 14
Aquinas High School, Bronx, NY

To me a best friend is everything,
My sunshine, my smile, my laughter.
A best friend is someone you can always talk to when you're
   down.
A best friend is always there for you, even when no one else is.
A best friend is always willing to listen and will never interrupt
   you.
I can't imagine life without a best friend.
A best friend is a gift.
Some friends may come and go,
but a best friend sticks with you through the good times and the
   bad.
A best friend can understand you and seems to know what you
   are feeling, and when you are feeling it.
One thing is for sure. I know who my best friend is. GOD.

Lauren, age 13
Saint Joseph School, Cottleville, MO

God has blond hair, brown hair, black hair, and red hair.
He is **TALL**, SHORT, **big**, and skinny.
She wears new clothes, old clothes, clean clothes, and dirty
   clothes.
He lives in a big house, small house, farmhouse, and mobile
   house.
She is plant and animal, sea and sky.
He needs love, happiness, hope, and understanding.
She is courageous, loving, caring, and free.
God is he or she in every person I see.

Jennifer Robinson, age 15
Assumption High School, Louisville, KY

Her voice in my head
gentler than the whisper
of a rosebud
under its breath
as it bends in harmony
with the grass and trees.
Her hair brighter
and more vibrant
than the kiss of the sun
upon the cheek of
the lakes and rivers.
Radiant beauty is hers,
unparalleled by any other,
though it is the basis for her creations.
Her eyes clearer and her
temperament calmer
than the sea after a storm.
From her I learned to treat
emotional frailty
not as a handicap but as a
minor obstacle.
She found in me inner strength
and brought forth my
own acceptance.
She cast aside my
temporary displacement,
and loved me as I was,
truly and eternally beautiful.

Jennifer Frey, age 17
Academy of Holy Angels, Richfield, MN

Some say God is an angry being,
with infinite power and might.
Some picture God as an old wise man,
dressed in robes of white.
Some think God is a force that comes
from deep within one's soul.
God, to me, is mother love,
sheltering children from the cold.

Courtney Schubert, age 17
Immaculate Heart Academy, Washington Township, NJ

The Lord is my director;
There is nothing I lack.
On lit stages you let me perform;
You restore my energy and strength.
You guide me to the right character.
Even when I stand alone in the spotlight, surrounded in
complete darkness, all eyes on me,
I fear no loss of lines for you are at my side;
Your confidence and encouragement give me endurance.
You set the stage before me
as my audience watches;
You bless my feet with grace,
my talent expands.
Only greatness and the power to tell others' stories will
pursue me all the days of my life;
I will act on the stage of the Lord for years to come.

Melissa Rae Poston, age 18
Queen of Peace High School, Burbank, IL

Who Is God for Me?

There is a certain feeling to stepping up to the plate, getting your signal, and eyeing up the pitcher. You steadily watch the fastball leave the pitcher's hand and enter the strike zone. You feel yourself turn your hips and crank the ball over the centerfield fence. You hear the crowd go wild and cheer frantically. Imagine the sensation you get when you round first base, the satisfaction you feel as you cross home plate. And you look at the crowd and see the proud expression upon your dad's face. The feeling of determination leads to accomplishment. God is the home run in the ninth inning when the count is 3–2, there are two outs, the bases are loaded, and the entire game is riding on your last hit. God is the game.

Dana M. Schiffman, age 17
Mount Carmel Academy, New Orleans, LA

God,

You're my air when I can't breathe.
You're my eyes when I can't see.
You're my strength when I am weak.
You're my mind when I can't think.
You're my love in times of hate.
You're my friend that's not fake.
You're my warmth when I am cold.
You're love that will never grow old.
God, you are my mind, body, and soul.
Amen.

Krystal Finocchiaro, age 11
Christ the King School, Rochester, NY

In the unity of a friendly gathering,
the encouragement from a loved one,
the courtesy of a stranger,
and the consolation of a friend,
we find comfort.

In the freshness of dewy grass on spring mornings,
the creativity of human works,
the independence of a sapling in the wood,
and the brilliance of the human spirit,
we find beauty.

In the happiness of the body after rest,
the excitement of new discovery,
the remembrance of something forgotten,
and the solitude accompanied by daydreams,
we find joy.

And still, in the power of the human mind,
the purification of a soul,
and the freedom offered by faith,
we find grace.

These are lovely, overlooked incidents
in a world where
the bad is the expected
and the good is a rarity.

Find courage in these God-given gifts
because they are love.
Remember that we always will be
the object of God's affection.

Shannon Leigh Nys, age 16
Academy of the Holy Cross, Kensington, MD

Prayer to God, Our Mother

O God, you are so loving and caring.
You are like a mother who loves and cares for her children.
As a mother gives birth, gives life to her children,
You give life to all creatures.
Like a mother in childbirth, you cry out in pain when we sin,
but only because you love us so much.
A nursing mother cannot go far if she forgets her child,
You, God, will never forget us.
You are our mother.

Like the eagles carefully guide their young, with a wing to fall
    back on,
You are our guide, God. We fall back on you.
A mother hen gathers her chicks to protect them from harm.
You hold us together in your arms of love, keeping us from any
    danger.
You are like the woman who searched for her lost coin, and
    rejoiced when she found it again.
When you lose us to earthly temptations, you search **high** and low
    for us, and sing praises in the sky when we come back to you.
You love us and care for us. You are too wonderful to put into
    words.
Amen.

Cassie Haupt, age 17
Queen of Peace High School, Burbank, IL

I recently went to a soup kitchen in Detroit, Michigan. I went
in part to find God. Surprisingly, God greeted me at the door of
the church we visited. He held a wonderful prayer service. Later,
as I entered the actual soup kitchen, I saw God again. She was
preparing some lunches in the back of the kitchen. He was

chopping lettuce and making meals. I washed tables later that day and suddenly I noticed God was right there beside me washing tables also! It was amazing how she was suddenly there. Some time later, God was sitting at one of the tables swinging his little feet that could almost touch the floor. Her rosy cheeks were stuffed with food, and his pudgy fingers reached for more. Her father's eyes, full of gratitude, were God's eyes. As it neared time to go, God came and went, he ate and he washed, she talked and he listened. As we left the kitchen, I began to worry that I would never see God again. All the way home, I worried that God would stay at that soup kitchen and never venture near my own house. When I got home I locked myself in my room and wept for my great loss. But then something amazing happened. As I passed a mirror I thought I saw God. I peered deeper into the mirror and realized it was! God was there inside my room, inside of me! I found that he had been there all along, and I didn't have to go to the soup kitchen to find him after all. But I'm sure glad I did.

Courtney Mullahy, age 16
Gabriel Richard Catholic High School, Southgate, MI

When you get to the point
when you can take control
of your energy
and transform it
into a positive one,
you have found
a special part of you . . .
GOD.

Frances Saunders-Malavé, age 17
Academia María Reina, San Juan, PR

"God, are you here?" I asked as I stood on a mountaintop, but only the cold wind answered me.
"God, are you here?" I asked again as I stood on the edge of a vast ocean, but only the crashing waves answered me.
"God, are you here?" I asked desperately as I stood in the stillness of a quiet forest, but only the rustling leaves answered me.
Finally, in despair, I cried in the silence of my heart, "God, where are you?" And in the silence of my heart, I heard a voice say, "I am here."

Lela M. Whitcomb, age 16
Saint Lucy Priory High School, Glendora, CA

God, you always have been, still are, and ever will be there for us.
When we come to a dark tunnel that is full of choices and decisions, you are always the light at the end of the right direction.
When we are caught in a storm full of torment and pressure, you are always the map with the arrow that points the way.
When we get stuck in a swamp of changes and adjustments, you are always the rope that pulls us out.
When we get overwhelmed by a parade of sadness, you are always the cloth that dries our eyes.
God, you always have been, still are, and ever will be there for us, for we are your children lost in a world full of conflict, choices, emotions, pressure, and changes. You are always the one with the hand that we hold as you walk us home. Amen.

Laura K. Goddu, age 13
Saint Raymond Parish, Dublin, CA

I sit very quietly with closed eyes,
And I feel it inside of me.
I call it God.
Others may call it Allah or Yahweh or merely just a presence,
But by whatever name I choose to call it,
It's that warmth that reaches out to me when I'm alone,
Keeping me from drowning in the cold waters of loneliness.
When happiness seems like nothing more than the vaguest
    glimmer on the horizon,
It pushes the sun high into the sky,
Lighting the darkness that once ruled within.
In the midst of a fight with one I love dearly,
And violent sobs rake through my entire body,
It's that gentle breeze that appears and dries the tears from my
    face.
When a peaceful calm pervades and all is quiet,
It's the beautiful sounds of songs unsung that whisper forth from
    that unique place inside.
But most important, it's the subtle urging in the back of my mind,
Constantly making me realize the profound beauty that is the
    core of life.

Ann Ehrhart, age 17
Villa Duchesne Oak Hill School, Saint Louis, MO

God
Powerful Creator
Heaven and Earth
Beyond our human understanding
Mystery

Kayla Hemmesch
Seven Dolors Parish, Albany, MN

God

God is within
All of the unending smiles of children,
All of the unexplainable giggles of happiness,
The precious fingers of a newborn baby,
The beautiful, bright shining moon,
The smell of the morning grass,
The sound of a newborn chick,
The feeling in a church,
God is there.

God

God is
The one who inspires me to continue,
Go beyond my hardships,
And reach for my dreams.
God is the key,
The door,
The mentor,
Waiting to be used,
Waiting to be called on and considered.
God does not demand perfection,
But effort,
God is everywhere.

God

God is
Love,
Compassion,
Generosity,
Wisdom,
Friendship,
God is life.

Stephanie Osborne, age 13
Saint John the Baptist School, Silver Spring, MD

The Story of Creation

The beginning of us
a birthday for her . . .

On the first day
there was light,
light of our creator,
a symbol of her guidance.

On the second day
there was painted
a portrait of her love,
a symbol of her grace.

On the third day
dry land was brought forth,
a place for a beginning,
a symbol of her hope.

On the fourth day
there was night and there was day,
four seasons too,
a symbol of her change.

On the fifth day
she fashioned birds to fly and fish to swim,
watching over us,
a symbol of her help.

On the sixth day
she molded animals to crawl on her earth,
protecting us from danger,
a symbol of her care.

On the seventh day
she made people,
created in her image,
a symbol of her love.

Rebecca Jane Kreitzer, age 14
Saint Odilia School, Shoreview, MN

My God is my life
And leader.
My God is my faith
And forgiver.
My God is my strengthener
And helper.
My God is my whole life.

Nicole A. Lopez, age 12
Our Lady Help of Christians School, Los Angeles, CA

God is my father, a caring man who walks with me each and every day. God is my mother, a gentle woman who embraces me in the midst of my turmoil and strife. God is my sister, the little girl with whom I seem to always butt heads, but in the end I love as much as ever before. God is my brother, stirring up my mind and making me question his actions and choices. God is the spirit, the spirit in my soul that makes me shine. God is the courage to share the word of Jesus. That courage can only be found in putting total trust in God, because without a father, mother, sister, and brother, we are lonely and afraid in the face of the evil ways of the world.

Jamie Bennett, age 17
Mercy Academy, Louisville, KY

Though it may not always seem possible,
God can appear anywhere, in any situation.
God is here.

The innocence of children playing in the sand,
splashing in the waves, picture of peace.
God is here.

Jet black clouds, pounding hail, and flashing lightning,
Power outages, flooding torrents, night of chaos.
God is here.

A bright day in the park, green grass sprouting,
hibiscuses blooming, people strolling, scene of contentment.
God is here.

Cars rushing by, crummy cardboard signs,
proud humility, begging for change, sight of misfortune.
God is here.

Fans cheering loudly, the ability to play as a team,
good sportsmanship, an atmosphere of excitement.
God is here.

Pain and suffering, possibly death, no one to love,
no one to be loved by, view of depression.
God is here.

Eyes closing slowly, comfortable bed,
plans for tomorrow, a feeling of serenity.
God is here.

Vanessa Plugge, age 14
Saint Agnes Academy, Houston, TX

God is . . .

. . . family dinners at my grandparents' house—the whole
family frantically swatting towels at the smoke detector,
laughing because it went off all the time . . . when I still sat
at the "kid" table.

. . . the way my little sisters fit perfectly into my arms.

. . . the smell of burning leaves—the change of the seasons.

. . . socks still warm from the dryer, pulled onto my cold feet.

. . . my mother's smile—her playful, mischievous laugh.

. . . lying in bed next to my two best friends and feeling nothing but love, security, and contentment.

. . . the wisdom that comes after making bad decisions.

. . . a hello from gram—"hey Mary—oh, my Mary!" her hands
on my face, kiss, hug, kiss.

. . . the earth who keeps me grounded while letting my spirit
soar.

. . . my father's hand on my back—comforting me, guiding me
through life.

. . . the sound of the whispers between my cousin and I—
thousands of miles apart.

. . . the feeling I get inside of me from being so in love with
life.

. . . the thought of my grandmother's love—searching, stable,
unconditional.

. . . the way a look from any of those boys communicates a
friendship that is beyond words.

God is family dinners at my grandparents' house—the whole
family frantically swatting towels at the smoke detector,
laughing because it went off all the time . . . when I still sat
at the "kid" table.

Mary Ireland, age 18
Little Flower High School, Philadelphia, PA

I see God at home,
I see God in my mom and dad, and in my brother and sister.
I see God in my church and school through my pastor and
   teacher.
I see God through my friends at school.
I see God through my godparents.
I see God through my relatives.
But most of all I see God in me.

Lisa Ortner, age 12
Danbury Catholic School, Danbury, IA

sounds of love
in the
circles of life

Twenty-two and still Teaching

My friend just celebrated her twenty-second birthday yesterday. Looking back, it seems like just yesterday when we were given permission to ride our bikes around the entire block. We thought playing with dolls, creating forts, and eating Popsicles were the quality ways of spending time. My friend is mentally challenged, yet has taught me more about life than any teacher or textbook could teach. Having grown up with her, I no longer focus on what's on the surface; I have learned to see what is underneath. She feels frustration at concepts that are hard to deal with, and needs all the same things as any human being. God just decided to put her in a special casing. He knew she would be strong enough to withstand the jeers, rejection, and betrayal. God taught her early to renew herself in him who strengthens. My friend has taught many people how to look at simple tasks in a creative way. It's this outlook that helps to refocus our world one person at a time. Fortunately for us, she's always teaching with $^Sm_ile^S$ and words of encouragement or through prayer. Turn to God today for the grace to see through his eyes and look for something special in someone. Challenge yourself to alter your perspective toward your neighbor. Be God's hands and feet.

Christen R. Pierce, age 16
West Catholic High School, Grand Rapids, MI

I see God when I wake up in the morning, when my mom is there to help us stay up in the morning. I see God when I get in line with my friends for school, and when my teachers come out to bring us inside. But most of all I see it in my mother. Mom is always there to help us. Mom is there when we are hurt or upset. Mom is there when I'm happy. She's always there to tell me how good I look and how it would look better if I did this or change into that. Mom's always there to help me when I am sick. Mom is always there to cheer me on in games and to give me advice. My mom hung up a quote from Abraham Lincoln: "All that I am or hope to be I owe to my mother." I most definitely agree.

Sarah Medina
Immaculate Heart of Mary School, Saint Louis, MO

The blessing that God has given to me
has nothing to do with material things.
God gave me a blessing that so many don't see.
The blessing of a mother who simply loves me.
She sees me for who I am and what I can be
and helps me believe in my most impossible dreams.
Sometimes I may shout I hate you and slam doors
and think to myself she doesn't love me anymore.
Her love however is unconditional, unselfish, and true
and she keeps on saying I will always love you.
Although at times it may seem like I don't care
I will always need her and she will always be there.
God has blessed me in so many ways,
but the greatest blessing I see every day.

Olivia Celest Foster, age 15
Saint Agnes Academy, Houston, TX

Dear Mom,
I am sorry I yelled at you.
I just felt really blue.
Can we please just talk
and go for a walk?
What I said was really mean
and I bet you're thinking,
"She's not goin' to make it past fourteen."
Mom, I know you're always there
and that you care.
But I care about you also
and now I really feel low.
I prayed to God, to see what I should say.
He said, "Maybe you should ask how was your day,"
and I did . . .
And then came the look, "Who are you trying to kid?"
But I am not trying to kid you, as you think.
Please just talk to me and smile,
even if it is just for a while
because I miss you.
What I said was not true
and I'll always love you!

M. K., age 13
Christ the King School, Rutland, VT

I was given a gift.
I knew who it was from.
It didn't come wrapped in ribbons or bows,
but was sent from afar.
This extra-special gift included unconditional
respect and acceptance.
At first I didn't understand.
Then I knew the gift was friendship.
I cared about this person,
and this person cared about me.
The greatest lesson this person taught me
is happiness doesn't come from popularity,
but from inside,
and just being me.

Leah Johnson, age 13
Venerini Academy, Worcester, MA

My family is my inspiration. All of my family members are there to talk when something goes wrong or when there is something good going on. If I need to, I can talk to them about things that happened to me. We are a very close group of people who stay together for all times. These people are the most important people in my life. All my family members are special because ever since the day I was born, my grandparents, aunts, uncles, cousins, and brother and, of course, my parents have been watching over me, correcting my wrongs. They are there if I have disagreements and they say, "Katie, we understand how you are feeling, but don't take it too seriously, that may cause you more trouble." They are also there to say, "Great job," when I do something good. They are my special gifts from God.

Katherine Jean Stanczak, age 11
Saint James Academy, Totowa, NJ

Gentle Mother,
All your children in the world love you and are so grateful.

Thank you for the nurturing mothers in the world and the gift of life that will never be forgotten.

Thank you for the endurance and strength you give women during their sacrifice to bear a child, just as you sacrifice your life for us.

Thank you for giving the gift of life to women and carrying out your intentions of human beings on earth and bringing family to men and women.

Thank you for the mothers who watch over us, as a hawk watches over her young.

Thank you for giving me a mother who is strong and caring, just as you are.

Thank you for creating women who are all a part of children's lives, just as we are all children of God.

Thank you for the motherly protection in the world, just as you protect us.

Thank you for the unselfish women in the world who will lend a helping hand and be happy with what they have, just like you have.

Thank you for the mothers who help sustain the world and follow in what you have created.

Thank you for creating women with goals and for helping them to accomplish them.

Thank you for all the women in our life who shine like the light of you. Amen.

Lisa Marie LaPorta, age 18
Queen of Peace High School, Burbank, IL

My Mother

My mother made a decision.
My mother made a mistake.
My mother made a choice.
She chose not to abort me.
She chose not to feel the grief.
She chose not to take my life.
She knew she couldn't keep me.
She knew she had to keep me alive.
She knew she could give me a better life.
Loving people would take care of me.
Loving people would take me into their home.
Loving people would teach me
Everything they know about knowledge,
Everything they know about love,
Everything they know about life.
Showing me that they care,
Showing me that their love is unconditional,
Showing me that I have a better life.
Teaching me so that I will not make her decision,
Teaching me so that I will not make her mistake,
Teaching me so that I will know.
My mother is a hero though I do not know her.
My mother is my giver of life.
My mother is one who took the path that most do not.

Desiree' L. Daehnke, age 18
Immaculate Heart of Mary Parish, New Melle, MO

A teacher is many things.
A teacher is a fountain of knowledge, flowing abundantly.
The water in a teacher's fountain is fresh,
and ready to be given to others, every single day.
It is a fountain of pure, untouched water.
It is a thing that inspires us,
guides us, and nurtures our minds.
A teacher's fountain of knowledge never runs dry.
God would never let it run dry,
for it is far too substantial to all who drink from it.
A teacher's fountain is something wise,
something to be respected, and something of great beauty.
We, the students, are the creatures who drink from the fountain.
We grow and develop under the shade the fountain bears.
We depend on the fountain;
it is the birthplace of our hopes and dreams.
When we stray in the wrong direction, the fountain gently
but firmly brings us back to the right path.
A teacher's fountain is a thing of light,
the darkness will never affect it.
Yet the darkness is changed by the teacher's fountain immensely.
The dark emptiness is brought into the light,
and what is good in it is brought forth and exemplified.
A teacher's fountain is as ancient as the sea,
and every bit as powerful.

Lindsey Marie Wilson, age 14
Lake Michigan Catholic Middle School, Saint Joseph, MI

What You Mean to Me

You turned my darkness into light,
You made everything all right.
You picked me up when I was down,
You turned my life around.
If I didn't have you, what would I be?
A *blessing* is what you are to me.

When I needed you the most, you were there,
Even if it seemed like you didn't care.
When I didn't think I could make it another day,
You chased all my doubts away.
If I didn't have you, what would I be?
A *treasure* is what you are to me.

The world is full of many people, it's true,
But there is only one of you.
You fill my heart with love,
You're a God-sent gift from above.
If I didn't have you, what would I be?
An *angel* is what you are to me.

Lost and alone, I will no longer be,
Because you are here with me.
There is no reason to be sad,
You've taken away all the bad.
If I didn't have you, what would I be?
A *best friend* is what you are to me!

Katrina L. Troyer, age 15
Saints Philip and James Parish, Canal Fulton, OH

My Sister

She walks into the room.
A sunbeam crosses the floor.
She takes away the gloom
And in return asks for nothing more.

She puts a smile on my face
And never lets me down.
She'll give me herself any day
When no one else can be found.

She is my forever friend
Always there to help guide.
And in the very end
She may be the only one by my side.

She, with the heart so giving,
The gift from God so high,
With the love that keeps on living
She's my sister, always by my side.

Leanne Altiero, age 14
Bishop Guilfoyle High School, Altoona, PA

Dear Friend,

I hope soon to see
That God has sent you over to me.
I need to talk
Or maybe go for a walk.
But whatever I do
It needs to be
With you.

Kelly Lynn Murphy, age 16
Houghton, MI

I am inspired by the person I know I am. Sure, I can hope to someday be someone special, but the person I am today is the person who has the strength to become that special someone in the future. I have looked to many people for hope and inspiration, but the women I admire the most are my grandmother, who had the strength to overcome difficulties in her marriage; my mother, who continues to have the strength to raise newborns through college-age kids; and my cousin, who is on her own journey to extending her happiness with others, all found through the guidance of God. These women have taught me never to underestimate myself, and that the journey is just as fulfilling and important as the destination.

Tina Baguio, age 17
Springfield Catholic High School, Springfield, MO

There once lived a woman who was known in her town as "The Mother Teresa of Neola, Iowa." I would like to tell you of a moment involving this woman that I believe may have counted for a small miracle. It hadn't rained for months. The crops on the farm weren't nourished. If this dry period went on, she and her husband didn't know what they would do. So, she prayed. She prayed for three months that rain would come and bring life to their farm. Still, it did not rain. Then, on April 27, 1996, this "Mother Teresa" left this world—and it rained all day. The rain poured down as if it hadn't rained for years. It was a gift from God—a sign that God had been listening all along. It was a miracle—a miracle for an angel's prayers. This angel was my grandmother.

H. J. C., age 17
Mercy High School, Omaha, NE

Women
Past — Present — Future

Woman was not a powerful word before.
No one's head would turn when a girl walked through the door.
They were not considered strong, independent, or even daring.
Women were always supposed to be motherly, loving, and most
    of all, caring.
Now things have changed.
Since Amelia, the first woman to fly a plane,
and Rosa Parks, who stood for her rights because she knew that
    it was only sane.
With those strong women and many more,
they were the women who opened many doors.
For the power of God was shown through all of them;
God showed them they were created equal to men.
So each little girl that reads this now,
Show the one who created you that you are **strong** and *proud.*
Let the women in the future be heard and always taught,
that many other women have paved the way,
to let all little girls be heard and have a say.

Beth Cunningham, age 17
Towson Catholic High School, Towson, MD

Some people come into our lives and quickly go. Some stay for a while and leave footprints on our hearts. And we are never, ever the same.

—Author unknown

God is all around us. He's in the people we encounter every day. The quote above best describes one person I encountered. Her name is Samantha.

It was an ordinary Saturday, and I was going to get my hair cut. My sister and I walked into the salon and we heard a voice call out, "Are you guys twins?" "Yes," we both replied as I rolled my eyes. It took me only a short time to realize that the voice came from a girl about my own age. We sat down next to her. I noticed that the girl was fairly short because her legs didn't even touch the floor. Her arms and legs were extremely thin in contrast to her rather plump torso. Her short curly hair looked as if it was thinning. "Hi," she said, "My name is Samantha. What's your name?" "I'm Meagan." I replied.

At first we made small talk, asking the usual questions: "Where do you go to school? How old are you?" I found out that Samantha had a tutor who home schooled her, and she was fifteen. After a long, awkward pause she said, "If you were wondering, I have a brain tumor." I was surprised at her openness, sharing a rather sensitive subject such as this one, with a person she didn't even know. "Oh," I replied. Then she talked about her sister, her grandma, her dogs (one's name was Tweety), and her friends. Then she talked about her surgeries. I asked if they hurt and she said they did, in a rather nonchalant manner. We continued to talk about music, movies, and TV. Then her grandma came, and she left.

After she left I kept thinking about how brave she was and how she never once complained. She had a silent courage that I knew I lacked. If the situation were reversed, I probably would have given up hope and felt sorry for myself. She acted as if nothing was wrong with her at all.

Plato once said, "Be kind, for everyone you meet is fighting a harder battle." Samantha definitely was.

When she first started talking, I was just listening to be polite, but it turns out that she was helping me in a way I didn't realize until long after she left. She made me realize how lucky I am to be healthy. She gave me a new perspective on life. I haven't seen her since, and I probably never will see her again, but I will always remember our conversation, one ordinary Saturday.

Meagan Lauener, age 16
McAuley High School, Joplin, MO

The Perfect Place

I sometimes find myself asking where home is. What is home? I
   guess you can have very many homes, but mine is wherever
   my mother is. I thought I would never find myself saying this,
   but it's true. Wherever my mother is, that's where home is.
   My mother told me that once, and it's always stuck with me.
Home is where you can run to every time you have a problem.
My mother will always be that home.
Home is a place where you'll find yourself crying and then all
   of a sudden laughing until your stomach hurts.
My mother will always be that place.
Home is where you can talk about all your problems and know
   that they'll be kept safe.
My mother will always be that safe.
Home is a place where you know that the doors will be open
   for you twenty-four–seven.
My mother will always be that door.
Home is a way to get into those arms of comfort that will take
   away all the pain and suffering you're going through.
My mother will always be those arms.
Home is a place where you can hide during a storm.
My mother will always be that hiding place.
Home is where you can be comfortable and not worry about
   being judged.
My mother will always be that feeling.
Home is a place where you can always find the warmth you
   need to get through the coldest winter.
My mother will always be that warmth.
Home is a heart filled with love for you no matter if you've been
   good or bad.

My mother will always be that heart.
My mother is my home, and I will never change anything about
her. She's as perfect as can be.
My mother is a perfect place.
My mother is my home.

Dedicated to my mother with all of my love,

Malissa Garcia
Church of the Resurrection, Mesa, AZ

I walk into a room
    surrounded by darkness.
I create my own light
    bring brightness to others.
Joy is meant for giving
    to others
and seldom kept for yourself.

I hope that when I'm gone,
    my brightness will linger
and explode into stars
    to brighten our sky.

Lynnette Williams, deceased
Bishop Guilfoyle High School, Altoona, PA.

Lynnette was a senior when she was tragically killed in an automobile
accident on October 11, 1999. She is deeply and sadly missed by her
family, the faculty, staff, and students at Bishop Guilfoyle High School,
and all who were touched by her presence.

Mary
Katherine

She lies upon my bed,
Many sweet kisses on her head.
Sharing every breath with me,
Knowing things others don't see.

Staring into the heart of my youth,
She echoes out every lost tooth,
Every party, every trial,
Single tears, single smiles.

She knows not how much time has passed.
She knows only of that which lasts,
Of love and prayers,
Of hopes and fears.

And as I dreamed, she held me tight,
She whispered silent comfort through the night,
And when I woke in tears or screams,
She soundlessly turned nightmares to dreams.

Now as I grow up she wears the same dress,
She lifts away the pain and stress.
Her life will be my life's reflection,
My childhood doll of a sweet rose complexion.

Emily Smith, age 14
LaSalle Academy, Providence, RI

Listening
through
tears

Memories of Mama

My little baby girl hand
Wrapped around her big mommy hand.
My hand held safely in hers
And her Bible grasped in the other.
We walked that way,
Never knowing where.
And we talked and we laughed,
About what I don't remember.
We walked, and walked,
And my little baby hand got bigger,
And her big mommy hand got slowly older,
But still so beautifully new.
Her fingernails always perfect.
I try to fashion mine that way,
But they could never compare.
She wasn't feeling well for a while,
So she went to the doctor one day
And changed our lives forever.
I watched for my mama for a few days,
Wondering why she wasn't there.
Waiting for her to walk in the door
And say, "Come here, babe, look what I've got here."
And she would smile so big
As she handed me the gift she wrapped with such care.
Then I realized what everyone had been telling me.
My mama will never again walk through the door,
Pick me up, and **whis**per sweet nothings in my ear,
Hearing her voice I so long to hear.
But deep down inside me still,
She will walk through the door,
So I can once again be held
In her big mommy arms.

Amanda Stuckey, age 15
Saint Lawrence Catholic Parish, Milbank, SD

I wear you around my neck close to my heart.
I try not to forget your love when the pain wears off.
I remembered the good times when I saw you resting
In your heavenly sleep.
My heart skipped a beat when yours stopped.

I will never forget your hugs
Or your smile, the way you laugh.
Our home is not quite the same without your words.
I know nothing remains the same
But I sure wish it would.

I will miss you when I walk down the aisle in white,
I hoped to hear you say to my love,
"Take care of my little girl."
I will miss your hug at the sign of peace,
And our dance cheek-to-cheek that day.

I know that your love will last forever,
Just like mine.
I wear you around my neck,
Close to my heart.

Judy Zirkelbach, age 17
McAuley High School, Cincinnati, OH

The Last Ray

Hopelessness smothers the last shimmering ray of light.
Complete darkness fills me.
The creepy shadows playing tag on the wall terrify me.
The gut-wrenching screams and strange noises
make my heart stop.
Something brushes against my hand and I instantly
tense up, ready to fly.
I am crowned with despair and gloom cloaks me.
My mind races until it bounces off the wall.
I am not even courageous enough to cry out.
No tears come.
You slip in unseen, in the shadowy corner, opposite mine.
You whisper my name gently as you come nearer.
I sigh contentedly as you gather me up in your arms.
I smile as a ray of light penetrates the darkness
and fills the room, lighting up the illusions that held my fear.
I cannot see you but I feel you, comforting me and loving me.
Your hand slips into mine as we leave behind
the cavernous place and enter the sunshine.
The kingdom dances for joy and greets me
as I join the celebration.

Kelly Hatzenbihler
Saint Martin Parish, Center, ND

Thank you God, for
Curing me when I was sick,
Urging me on when I lost hope,
Picking me up when I fell,
Wiping my tears when I cried,
Sticking with me when I felt abandoned,
Calming me when I got angry,
Feeding me with love when my heart grew hungry,
Comforting me when others put me down,
Being with me when I knew nobody but loneliness,
And always being my friend through the storms
and sunshine you blessed me with.

Emily Ko, age 14
Saint Elizabeth Ann Seton Parish, Irvine, CA

As Time Goes By

Every day, as time goes by,
I think, "Why did my dad have to die?"
Age thirteen is too young to know
how it feels when a parent must go.
I lie in my bed crying, with a pain in my heart,
Why are my father and I apart?
I am scared for my mom, my brother, my friends.
What would I do if their lives were to end?
I pray to God that no one else will die,
Every day, as time goes by.

Abby, age 13
Catholic Church of Ascension, Hurricane, WV

I Love You and Good-Bye

I looked into her eyes,
eyes that would always sparkle,
eyes that were always joyful,
but now they just stared back at me.

I looked into her face,
a face that would always shine,
a face that would always smile,
but now it was cold and dry.

I looked into her heart,
a heart that was filled with happiness,
a heart that was healthy and strong,
but now was filled with sorrow.

I looked at her,
a beautiful grandma who always loved me,
a grandma who wanted to help,
but now she needed help.

I looked at my grandma,
once a grandma that helped me,
once a grandma that comforted me,
but now a grandma that I had to comfort and help.

I looked at my grandma,
so sad and starry-eyed,
needing help, help the doctors couldn't give,
help that only God could give.

I looked at her and cried,
not knowing what would happen next,
not knowing what to do,
I looked at her and said, "I love you and good-bye."

Caroline Eccleston, age 13
Visitation Academy, Saint Louis, MO

Strength in God

Sometimes you have to be strong and stand up for yourself when no one else will. You have to stand your ground and pass it off as another lesson learned. Your pains turn to sorrows and soon heal with time. But pain will only heal if you let it. If you dwell on it, time will bury it deep in your heart and a bitter hatred will come. A hatred only God can heal with love. When God's love comes over you, you let go. Tears drop from your eyes like bombs, and you fall into the arms of a friend and tell her all about it. After you let go of your hatred, you get up, dust yourself off, and stand strong once again, under the wing of God.

Joanna E. Gunther, age 15
Saint Joan Antida High School, Milwaukee, WI

If only my will could be stronger,
My voice louder.
I spend my nights awake
And my days wandering,
Searching but never finding.
I know not what I'm looking for
A friend
A mother
A father
A plug to fill the hole,
The void.
I need someone,
Something
Much more than I have.
Could this be God?

Janelle C. Barnette, age 17
Immaculate Heart Academy, Washington Township, NJ

Emmanuel

Feeling anger, hurt, and sadness.
Why do I feel so lost, so lonely, so tired?
I know not what I will become;
Where are all the happy times I felt as a child,
When I felt secure and loved?
Why do I not feel like that now?
Why am I always angry inside?
My life feels awry.
I don't feel I control it anymore.
How can I make things better?
I know that removing myself from this world is not the answer,
But is that the only thing that will make me happy?
As I'm sitting here, I feel a light begin to shine inside of me,
I feel someone comforting me, consoling me,
Soothing my depression.
I begin to feel lighter, and the waves of my hurt
Disappear, evaporate.
The weight of my depression is lifted from my shoulders,
And I realize that God is with me.

Domenica Bongiovanni, age 15
Notre Dame de Sion High School, Kansas City, MO

Dear God,

You saved my life today. Everything was causing me pain—tests, projects, papers due, teacher and parent conflicts, friend problems, and so on. I didn't want to stay here, I wanted to escape from it, fast. I sat in my room today with a bottle of aspirin in one hand, and a glass of water in the other. I started taking in the aspirin, in hopes it would make the pain go away. I was taking a seventh pill, when my phone rang. I answered it, and it was you, God, acting through my friend. She asked me if anything was wrong because I had seemed pretty sad lately. I hesitated, but all I said was "No." I looked at the bottle and glass, but I just left them there. I sat on the floor, thinking. Thank you, God, for saving my life.

Grace Lorenzo, age 17
Notre Dame Academy, Los Angeles, CA

Letting Go

Lately it seems
I crumble like a leaf
being broken down by the wind.

Shed more tears
than I have spread smiles,
praying soon that there will be an end.

Doubt and confusion
have a part in me,
suddenly I have grown cold.

Hope and love
rule over me
and always your hand is there to hold.

I am afraid
but you walk beside me
and hard today becomes bearable tomorrow.

I will know
because you will guide me
and slowly every day more pain will be let go.

Melissa Renee Bagneris, age 17
Cabrini High School, New Orleans, LA

Lord,
Grant me the clarity to know that when trials arise, I can perse-
vere, for you would never give me more than I could handle.
And let me realize, O Lord, that in times of strife, I am not alone,
that my tears are cried by two, that my pain is endured by
another, and that you hold me in an eternal embrace that can
never be broken. Amen.

Olivia-Marie Villanueva, age 17
Saint Lucy Priory High School, Glendora, CA

I Am

I am the sister of a handicapped child.
I wonder if people can ever see him for who he is.
I hear the whispers of onlookers.
I see people staring.
I want him to have everything I have.
I am the sister of a handicapped child.

I pretend sometimes that he is normal.
I feel the pain inside my heart.
I touch the heavens and ask for help.
I worry about when his life will end.
I cry when I see the pain in my stepfather's eyes.
I am the sister of a handicapped child.

I understand why people may view him differently.
I say they will get over it.
I dream that he will be able to live past the age of twelve.
I try to hold on to the belief that he will get better.
I hope for a cure.
I am the sister of a handicapped child.

Jamie Ressie, age 16
Cochrane, WI

Life?

Questions go unanswered;
thoughts kept quiet.
Actions go unseen;
words are never heard.
Love goes unfelt;
heart stays EMPTY.
This is my life;
who is God again?

Amy Osterman, age 15
Regina High School, Harper Woods, MI

All you ever did was laugh and play,
But that all changed in just one day.
You hear she died, you have nothing to say;
You start to cry and want to run away.
Now, you never laugh and you hate to play.
The pain you thought would go away, you realize is here to stay.
You cover the pain, you tell everyone you're fine,
You think they believe, but they are not blind,
They see you're hurt, they want to be there,
They will help you with your pain and show you they care,
They are the ones who will never dare
To let you deal with pain and not make you share.
They are your family, your friends, your life.
Trust me, I've lived through that day.
Those people are why I am able to say,
that I am still here today and planning to stay.

Angelia Guglielmo, age 17
Archbishop Mitty High School, San Jose, CA

Friendships Gone, but Not Forgotten

After you moved away,
I thought we'd be closer than ever.
I tried so hard to keep what we had,
but I noticed phone calls were less,
and their contents almost empty, not completely full.
Everyone told me we weren't best friends anymore.
I tried to prove them wrong,
but in the end they were right.

I'm having a tough time right now,
I need to talk to you,
but I can't seem to anymore.
I feel like a bore to you.
Why, oh why can't it be the same?

The other day I realized,
we can't be as close,
but we can still talk.
I wish it could be the same,
but that's what life is all about.
Growing up can be hard,
but it's something we all go through.
Friends will come and go,
but I'll always remember you,
and keep you close to my heart.
I love you, and I always will.

Alison Webb, age 14
Christ the King School, Rutland, VT

Dear Grandpa,
I wish you were here
by my side.
I miss you so.
Remember when
I sat on your lap and watched
the Cubs baseball game.
Those were the good times.
Now I am older and there are times
when I really need you.
I wish I could see your face
so warm and thoughtful.
I wish I could have given you
a hug before you left.
To me it would have meant a hug forever.
I wish you could have just
held on a little longer.
I had so many important things
for you to hear.
But now I will just have to wait
until I see you again.

Kara Kay Pithan, deceased
Saint Mary Parish, Danbury, IA

*Kara wrote this poem about her grandfather in November 1999. On 27
December 1999—twelve days after her sixteenth birthday—she was killed
in an automobile accident.*

Innocence Lost

Now I can see,
and I am no longer naïve.
The blinders have been taken away,
and I am free.
Yet I am trapped.
Trapped between good and evil,
between standing up and turning away.
For now I see the hate,
now I see your scorn.
I am no longer so blinded by innocence,
but aware by guilt.
Guilt for not stopping the bad,
the words, the punches, the knives.
Guilt for turning away,
for never believing things were bad.
But now I am old,
no longer naïve.
I see you and your hateful ways.
I see your scorn.
But through this I will be strong,
I will not succumb to the hate,
for I believe in good.
I will survive my journey,
with God by my side.
My journey from naïve baby,
my journey to find me.

Seanne Casey, age 14
Mount Mercy Academy, Buffalo, NY

each day, another day to live on
candy-coated lies
sweetness trapped in my throat
can i breathe on?
drowning in a sea of my own tears
caught in the envelope i sealed myself
am i lost?
all of them expecting me to "find" you
you who are "you?"
"i am the voice inside your head"
    "i am the truth from which you run"
        "i give you all you need to know"
all i need to know? i know so little, i want more . . .
maybe i am asking too much,
are these thoughts impure?
denial   **guilt**   *fear*
i am afraid to see
    to be part of that lamb
am i worth someone dying?
            (would i die for this?)
why is it such a kingdom of pain and death and suffering?
i guess i just find the faults to hide my own
maybe i am the only threat, myself, the chaos, not within you
but in me
until it all ends, i will hide
hide from everything
maybe by hiding i can find you, like they said
or maybe
        you could find me

Holly Mendenhall, age 15
Marymount High School, Los Angeles, CA

Help Me

Oh God, please help me with this anger.
Every time it happens it is something new.
It's an ocean unexplored that
Cannot be tamed or touched by anyone.
Please help me in rough times, for I know you will.
I cannot control myself when it happens,
It's a disturbance of my inner peace,
I am being violated.
It screeches for help,
But others can hear nothing
Except for me.
Please console me, for I cannot let anyone in
Until you can.

Erica M. DeArmas, age 15
Saint Mary High School, Jersey City, NJ

When a House Is Not a Home

When a house is not a home
The kids get left alone,
Do whatever they want,
Don't know how to react,
Mamma strung out on crack,
Daddy nowhere to be found,
No wonder why they frown. . . .
The kids behave like little clowns.
It's not their fault they're all messed up.
When they grow up, there's nowhere to go,
But the opposite of up.

LaQuitta, age 18
Benedictine High School, Detroit, MI

One Who Made Us

When happiness turns to fears
We as humans shed tears
Believing there's a greater power, I pray
Asking for a better day.
Riots, "no justice—no peace," voices ring.
Is the one who made us contemplating
Whether to end it because through these walls
Lie departed souls
Who died with unjust cause?
Wanting to stop it but time cannot pause.
Silently approaching dying days
Parents of pregnant teenage girls say it's just a phase.
What happened to waiting for marriage?
My peers left pushing a baby carriage.
Trusted to protect us but tearing down our rights
Playing with lives as yet another one dies.
What a tragedy, mothers bury sons.
I say, strip them of their guns.
Sitting here waiting, still no rainbows
Is the one who made us looking down disappointed?
Because the good die young and God knows.

Tiberah Tsehai, age 17
Saint Mary High School, Jersey City, NJ

The Angel

I had noticed her before,
She was different from the others.
Her mind had learned much.
Her hands had toiled hard.
You could get a glimpse of life
At its fullest and most grand
Just by looking in the sweet glowing warmth
Living within her eyes.
The sadness had engulfed me
Hid me from the light.
It was a darkness,
My mother's death,
An everlasting night.
Wandered through the streets
My mind still in shadow.
Then I saw her reaching to me
with her arms of love and strength.

The soul.
The mind.
The feelings of the heart.
These were known to her.
I could feel it from the start.
Then her words flowed over me
Washed away the night:
"Don't worry, child. God works through me.
It's gonna be all right."

Then gone.
She vanished
And only her words would remain:
"Don't worry, child. Your mom's with God.
It's gonna be okay."

The presence of God
Filled the gap within my soul.
We will not,
Not one of us,
Ever be alone.

Angela Lee Toole, age 13
Saints John and James School, Ferguson, MO

Losing a Friend

O Messenger of the light,
Tell me you have good news.
Another life is lost and all because of what?
One more piece of happiness, taken from the earth
And spread across the heavens to brighten the angels.
Why should I just weep in torment after this lost soul?
Shouldn't I climb to the highest mountains and **scream?**
Shouldn't I curse this blackness that has come over me?
O please, Holy Light,
Tell me that there is a better plan for this blessed soul;
That you will put her back on this earth,
If not for me, then for someone else.
Allow her to spread happiness here
Instead of making her stay in the clouds above
To be only admired instead of received.
O God,
I know you will do what you think is best,
But give this soul a chance to shine happiness
Into someone else's heart and mind as much as she has mine.

Gerri Brackett, age 15
Loretto High School, Sacramento, CA

I Go to God

When all the world has left me
And I'm standing all alone,
When the people I depended on
Have turned and walked away,
My heart is breaking in two.
I just want to fall apart.
Suddenly I know where to go.
I know who will lead me in the fight.
I fall onto my knees
Before my God
Who gives wings to my soul
And fills my heart with hope.
I know that I've been held
By a force I cannot see
And so I can keep on going
To meet another day.

Shana Kay
Mother of Mercy High School, Cincinnati, OH

Driving into the Darkness

Every day and every night
I scream out until my throat bends and bleeds.
No one hears me.
 Pain has to go someplace; it's buried deep in my heart,
  No scrape or cut could make it all pour out.
 Thought I had my life strapped tight into my backpack,
  Until it snapped up and opened on me.
  S
     p
       i
         l
           l
             i
               n
                 g
     Over all of
     My thoughts up till the point
     Where I was but soot and ash.
My mind wanders into interregnum
And tends to stay there until someone snaps me out of it.
It's not easily managed or controlled, I've adapted to it.
I face all my fears, likes, and dreams of utmost desire of what
My heart longs for.
Breaking away from this world into another.
Each time I fight I lose myself
                              Bit by bit.

Slowly disintegrating into a nothingness . . .
Forgive me God as I drive on into the darkness.

Rachel Pastick, age 14
Saint Odilia School, Shoreview, MN

Hate

An ember flickering in their eyes
The all-consuming wrath of hate
Flaming to destroy their Savior.
A pierced palm and a punctured heart
The final propitiation
For our eternal salvation.
They closed their eyes to the truth
Denying him as deity
The sacrificial lamb for all,
Sodden with the crimson of my sin.

Natalie Ann Houston, age 16
Blessed Trinity Catholic Community, Orlando, FL

Murmurs
of creation

Morning Prayer

The sun rises again
The first vision
A revelation
The coming of a new dawn
Setting the sky ablaze like fire
Clouds of wool
Over a lamp stand.
Trumpeting birds
Air rushing like water over my skin
GoOseBumPs
Only seven stars left in the sky
Lamp stands of their own
Never fading through the day.
The warmth of a furnace embraces me.

The sun is the first and the last and lives on and on. . . .
It once was dead during the night
But now it lives again forever and ever.
The sun has risen.

Praise God for the revelation.

Shea, age 16
Holy Family Catholic Community, Middletown, MD

Thunderstorm

The past, present, and future
Lives in the rain.
The water grumbles in the belly of the sky,
Then cascades out of its mouth,
Sometimes with the aid of thunder and lightning,
Other times alone in its own race.
It then touches the earth,
Who, in turn, drains it and makes a home
For it,
Either in its womb or in the seas.
More time passes, and the water
Rises into the atmosphere,
Slowly, in a crystal-like process.
Clouds gather the water into their open arms,
Until sky bangs on its drum
In the coming of its stomachache,
And the storm lives once more.
I cannot help but take comfort in this;
Such a mystical and essential cycle repeats itself
Over and over and over
Again!

Lindsey W., age 14
Saint Elizabeth High School, Wilmington, DE

By the Beach

I walk along the beach, picking up seashells in the sand,
Breathing in the salty coolness of the morning.
I take careful steps with the waves curling at my feet below.
And the motion eases me of my fears.
As the cool waves breathe in and out, they wipe away the
   footprints of yesterday.
And the dampness from the ocean air clings to my shirt like a
   baby to its mother.
Small colorful periwinkles burrow into the sand leaving no sign
   of their existence,
And seagulls call to one another as the morning rises.
The sun streaming through the windows summons sleeping
   people with its promise of warmth.
While I walk, everything is waking to a new day with a perfect
   beginning.
I hear the chatter of people in the distance; the day has begun.
The morning tide rises; I realize it is time to return home.
Tomorrow morning will come, and the beach will call me once
   more—allowing me to walk in the beauty of God.

Emily Moores, age 15
Mother of Mercy High School, Cincinnati, OH

God All Around Me

Waves crashing,
wind whispering,
shells shimmering,
Life all around me.

Worms crawling,
raindrops falling,
flowers growing,
Love all around me.

Birds singing,
chipmunks running,
butterflies fluttering,
Faith all around me.

Blue sky above me,
brown earth beneath me,
green trees near me,
Belief all around me.

Humans new, old,
black, white, yellow, tan,
boys, girls, men, and women,
God all around me.

Beth Vitaris, age 12
Venerini Academy, Worcester, MA

Baptism Rain

Water trickles down my body
Washing the spirit and soul
Creating something to make one
Creating a cleansing of the world.
As the water falls from the sky
I sit and wonder why
The sky must turn so gray
For such a beautiful rain.

KC Andrews, age 16
Saint Gertrude High School, Richmond, VA

Chilled winds still flow through the air,

as starlight gazes on the sleeping surface.
Moonshine starts to disappear,
    while life begins to emerge.
The birds sing their sweet, early song
    and the sun sheds increasing warmth,
        warmth onto what seemed to be a dead, cold day.
Extreme colors appear in the sky above,
    blue, orange, red, brought out by the rising sunlight.
Soon the warmth reaches its peak
    and all signs of the night have vanished.
Light emerges in awe, and life awakens.
The morning,
    so pure, so beautiful
and another day has begun.

Stephanie, age 17
Villa Duchesne Oak Hill School, Saint Louis, MO

Where I Saw God

I
grew
in a garden
where the sun rained down,
and
the rainbow shimmered
against the whitewashed sky.

I
flew
in the forest
where the chipmunks chattered,
and
the trees shined like emeralds.

I
walked
among the people
where I took their hands
and
learned them,
and
I
saw
the love in their eyes.

I
drifted
on the waters
where I saw myself
and
where I saw God.

Greta Hansen, age 15
Saint Bartholomew Parish, Wayzata, MN

Masterpiece

My Lord, my God
Creating such beauty.
Sparkling waters:
Oceans, rivers, lakes.
Overpowering trees:
Pine, oak, maple.
Gentle and powerful creatures:
Chipmunk, lion, squirrel
Bear, rabbit, wolf,
And us—
To enjoy all the glories of your masterpiece.

Emily Hildenbrand, age 13
Academy of Notre Dame de Namur, Villanova, PA

Nature has always been a place where I have experienced God. God's presence is evident in the wind that gently sweeps the leaves and the sun that trickles down, creating patterns of light upon the forest floor. I am greatly reminded of my spirit's growth whenever the passage of time elapses into the next season. Autumn, when the trees shed their leaves, is a reflection of the sloughing of my sinful ways before the dormancy of winter, where my sins are set to an eternal sleep. With spring I am reborn—given another chance at life—just as the trees awake from their slumber to unfold verdant new leaves. Summer marks the period of maturity. The branches of my inner spirit expand to their fullest potential. Just as the trees grow toward the light, I, too, continue to grow—always reaching upward, striving for the eternal light of heaven.

Kimberly Zukowski, age 16
Saint Mark High School, Wilmington, DE

Winding Roads

I walk this winding path looking for you.
The golden trees sway above me,
the gentle breezes blow around me,
The animals scatter and flutter all about me,
As I walk along this winding path looking for you.
I seek you to speak to me,
but in my eyes you are not to be found.
I am frustrated and all of a sudden you are there.
I see you, I feel your presence
in the trees, breezes, and all around.
I hear you, God, your voice, in that of the animals.
You speak to me.
You comfort my weary spirit.
You put my mind and heart at rest.
I thank you, God, thank you for guiding me.
Then you are gone.
You are near to catch me if I stumble over a bump in the road,
but you let me walk on my own.

Sharon E. Szafranski, age 15
Magnificat High School, Rocky River, OH

*Listen to the music in the sunrise. Feel the colors flowing
across the sky. Look at the breeze embracing all in its path.*
Life is a book. Jesus is the author, God is the illustrator, and we
are the characters that play the roles. In the great book of life,
everyone's destiny is not to have a destiny.
*Listen to the music in the sunrise. Feel the colors flowing
across the sky. Look at the breeze embracing all in its path.*
Have no fear, for God is here.

Caitlin Duncan, age 12
Sacred Heart Academy, Redlands, CA

A shell rests in the sand.
A wave reaches the shore
And grabs the shell to carry it away.
The shell fights to stay on the beach,
But surrenders to the water.
The waves capture her,
Turn her,
Command her,
And the shell loses sight of the sand.
She is lost.
But then something happens.
The Creator dips a hand into the sea
And helps her change direction.
She can see the shore again.
She rejoices.
And then a huge wave hurls the shell back onto the sand.
She secures herself on the beach.
Another wave comes
And tries to take the shell away again.
But this time she remembers the One
Who dipped a hand into the sea
And changed her path toward home.
And so the shell holds on tighter.
The wave seems weaker than the tiny shell.
She fights off the waves.
Now she is home.

Julie Marie LaBelle, age 17
Saint Joseph Academy, Saint Louis, MO

At the Ocean

sitting on the soft sand
I contemplate my spirituality.
watching the cool
blue water crashing
over the shiny rocks
I think about the ones that I love
my family, friends, teachers,
they all give me hope
hope in life,
hope to do
what I think is good.
they are always there for me
if I need inspiration.
so I sit here
thinking,
watching as the sun's rays
shine on me.
the ocean
gives me hope.
here at the ocean
I can think
about what I value most
my friends, family, teachers.
I stand up
as the wind breezes
through my golden locks.
I go to be
with the people I love,
value,
and cherish
every second.

Emily Baebler, age 15
Saint Gertrude High School, Richmond, VA

And God Was There

The cold, hard crying winds trudged,
A dusting snow softened the lands,
And God was there to be sure the snowflakes were all unique.

Then joyful rain showers skipped,
The cooling drops refreshing the earth,
And God was there to be sure they would make flowers bloom.

The golden rays came tumbling down,
And cheered the earth inside and out,
And God was there to be sure traveling feet were soothed.

Then air so crisp went running about,
And painted the leaves so bright, bright red
And God was there to be sure only the best paints were used.

Wherever you go, God will walk with you,
and make sure the ground on which you tread is
softened, refreshed, warmed, and only the best.

Victoria Jean Novak, age 13
Saint Robert School, Shorewood, WI

As I gaze into the stars,
I see a life that was lost.
They lead me to you,
And then I can see you.

Sometimes I spend hours looking for you,
When I find the brightest star,
I know it is you.
You are smiling back at me.

There is so much I want to tell you.
All I have to do is go outside and look up.
I am thankful for the stars.
Through them, I see you.

Elizabeth Lauren LaBarbara, age 15
Saint Joan of Arc Parish, Jackson Heights, NY

Sometimes I stop and just look at the trees,
So tall, strong, and godly, yet bushy and brave.
In the branches above me, birds continue to flee,
Every little while to a different place.

I settle back and watch the squirrels gathering nuts,
The robins chirping in the trees,
And my heart sings praise for God,
Who created all of these.

As I tilt my head to the heavens,
And I feel the need to give thanks,
As I watch the gold-red sun sink gently behind the trees,
Then the quilt of darkness falls for all to see.

Shannon Ryan, age 12
Holy Family School, South Pasadena, CA

The Call

A walk in the woods,
A voice in the wind,
God calling me
to see the light.
I climb a tree
and draw what I see.
The quiet, trickling river,
The bridge squeaking softly,
The solid tree,
the water-covered rocks,
And then I see God's
footsteps in the mud.
Again I hear God,
who calls me to be an artist.

Amy Piersak, age 14
Saint Odilia School, Shoreview, MN

I saw a small bunny

build a fancy nest
Getting ready for her babies;
    she wanted them to have the best.
She worked hard day and night
    preparing for their birth.
When at last they arrived
    she knew what it was worth.
For only our Creator
    in heaven up above
Could teach that simple bunny
    that new life grows in love.

Elizabeth Meringer, age 12
Our Lady of the Valley School, Wayne, NJ

Colors of My Heart

If I were red, I would be the breast of a robin flying swiftly to my nest.

If I were yellow, I would be a newly hatched chick opening my eyes to the newfound world.

If I were orange, a wing of the monarch soaring toward the blazing harvest moon.

And if I were green, I would be an evergreen mysteriously swaying with the ever-changing wind.

Being the blue mist around a full moon on a cold winter night would certainly be nice.

If I were indigo, I would be the sunset on the last day of spring, shattered in thousands of pieces.

If I were pink, I would be a newborn piglet venturing out into the colorful world.

If I were brown, a slender worm weaving through the dark earth.

And if I were black, I would be a midnight sky cradling and brightening the resting stars in my quilt of shadows.

Lindsey Kristin Davis, age 13
Bellevue, NE

On a warm spring dusk, I look out upon the horizon and am witness to a glorious display of God's finest artwork—a sunset. The sun softens to a deep orange while cloaking itself in a sheet of color. The paints mingle amongst themselves, creating colors no other artist could blend on a palate: deep magentas, rich eggplants, and cool tangerines. As human clay hand-sculpted by God, I too am a magnificent creation. I am the most beautiful Me there is. I have been designed with unique talents and an unparalleled personality. Oh God, help me to recognize my inherent beauty and to reject all outside toxins which prevent me from cultivating and displaying my true beauty.

Molly Keegan, age 17
Saint Joseph Academy, Saint Louis, MO

Rainbow of Hope

When you are free
In mind and soul,
Dance on the stars
And fly in the air.
When you are happy,
Swim in the garden of hope
With the flowers of joy.
When you are worried,
Feel summer breezes
Blowing the clouds
Of your misery away.
When you are imagining,
Paint yourself a sunset
In the magic of spring.
When you are angry,
Picture a songbird
To sing you a story
of love and life.
When you are sad,
Bathe yourself in peaceful dreams,
And watch your tears melt away.
When you are laughing,
Fill your mind
With prayers of happiness.
When you are in need,
Pray to the soul of an angel.
Look to the colors of the rainbow for hope.
You'll always remember the happy times
And surround yourself with love.
You will listen to yourself.
When the storm of your years passes,
God will always be there to guide you.
God will always be there by your side.

Hope Elizabeth Cannon, age 13
Catholic Community of Saint Charles Borromeo, Skillman, NJ

Dear God,
Please speak to me. Speak to me through raging winds. Speak to me through strong ocean waves. Speak to me through the swaying grains of the fields. Speak to me through the obstacles I face. Speak to me through the people I love. Speak to me through my heart and my soul. God speak to me and help me listen to your words.

Caitlin Reynolds, age 12
Saint Francis of Assisi School, Saint Louis, MO

Dear Wind,
Every time I feel you against my face and in my hair, I think of the love of God. Every time I witness your force and strength, I think of the greatness of God. When I see you sway flowers in the gentle breeze, I think of the beauty of God. When I hear you hitting my window on a windy night, I think of the protection offered by God. Wind, you have the power to be beautiful, gentle, forceful, and mysterious. I can't see you, but I know you're there. You remind me of God's beauty, grace, force, power, gentleness, and love. I've never seen God, but when I hear the leaves rustling with the wind, I know God is right beside me. When I go to the beach, and see the sand in an uproar with the wind's power, I know God is looking down on me. When I hear the wind whistle with joy at night, I know God is singing me to sleep. When I see the birds glide with your gentle help, I know God always has a shoulder for me to lean on. When I see you create ripples on even the most giant lake, I know I have the power to change the world through God's help. Wind, you remind me of God in all that you do. It is because of you that I have had the opportunity to know, love, see, and feel God.

Kathleen Lynch, age 17
Holy Angels Academy, Demarest, NJ

God's Works

Across the sky-blue spaces,
Across the endless skies,
With showering of mighty wings,
The wind of God goes by.
"Peace in God's name," they whisper,
"Peace in God's name," they cry.
People do you not hear
The wind of God go by?
Above the mountains,
With unseen sandals shod,
Above the plains, with lots of rain,
Swept by the winds of God
What are wings but flesh and bones
And flashing feathers, these alone . . .
Bear the sparrow, wild and free
From the lowest earth to hilltop tree.
These alone lift the hawks and blue jays
To a world of endless sunny days,
Of the lizard and the hare,
Or the panther in his lair.
What are wings? They are to me
Soundless songs and poetry
Carved, wherever wild birds fly
On the fresh page of that sky.

Kim-Van Tran, age 15
Saint Joan Antida High School, Milwaukee, WI

I hear trees
Whispering softly
I love you.
The stream gurgles
You are special.
Mountains echo
I care, I care.
The wind shrieks
Come to me.
I sit here surrounded by God,
Who is everywhere.
My God is in my soul.
Just listen.
Shhh.
Listen.

Ellie Bassindale, age 12
Saint Robert School, Shorewood, WI

Conversations
with God

Dear God,
Where are you?
Where have you gone?
I know that you are there, everywhere,
But I cannot see you.
You are in my heart, but my eyes are not certain.
You tell me to believe, but how can I know for sure.
Please show me the way.

Katie Johnston, age 12
School of the Holy Child, Rye, NY

I immerse myself in your splendor
In your beauty I am lost.
The skies speak of your wonders
And the mountains tell of your majesty.
A breath of a gentle breeze inebriates my soul
With your gentle truth.
I lift my eyes toward the heavens, the haven of my soul
For it is where my love awaits me,
It is your home.

Michelle Medina, age 17
Saint Peter and Saint Paul Parish, Alta Loma, CA

Dear God,
I'm scared.
I'm scared of what people will think of me.
I'm scared people will think I am strange.
I'm scared people will think I am a religious weirdo.
I love you, God, but I am afraid to show it.
I need you, God, but I am afraid to show it.
I say grace in the cafeteria, but quickly.
I genuflect at Mass, but when no one is looking.
Why?
Why do I need to hide my Christianity?
Why do I need to be afraid of what is important to me?
I don't know.
I must be strong.
I must be fearless.
I must be kind, thoughtful, generous, patient, respectful,
courageous.
But sometimes I can't.
I need you, God.
I need you to help me,
Be with me when I am scared.
Be with me when I am challenged.
Be with me when I need a little nudge.
Be with me when I need you.
I know you will.
Be with me, God, when I am scared.
I love you.

Kathleen Souder, age 15
Knoxville Catholic High School, Knoxville, TN

Inside

The questions inside me are deep,
The choices inside me are strong.
But your questions always sink deeper.
Your choices are never wrong.

I look to you for guidance,
I ask you for your help.
And your guidance is always perfect,
Your answers are always felt.

Lately my spirit has been falling,
Lately my heart has grown mild,
But you're always there to pick me up.
You love me enough to call me your child.

So don't judge me, like I do you,
Don't blame me for being me,
I know I am beautiful in your eyes,
And I know how loving you can be.

Alexandra Jabs, age 14
Rosary High School, Aurora, IL

There is a fire in me, God. This fire is the essence of who I am. It is my true hopes, visions, and fears, protected by my many layers from the outside world. It can be hard in these teenage years to peel back my layers through all the outside pressure and expose the core me. I yearn to discover my true self and embrace my unique gifts and talents. I know this is key to a fulfilling life and true happiness. I want to explore and achieve great things, and make use of everything the world has to offer me. God, you know me because you lovingly created me as an exceptional individual. Give me the courage to embrace the person you intended me to be so that through my optimism and burning passion for life, I may be a light for others.

Lisa Lachky, age 17
Saint Joseph Academy, Saint Louis, MO

Life, full of ups and downs
Given with a purpose from God.
Some, as I do, smile with happiness
And hold on to the good moments.
But some, as I also do, go to God
Only when they are blue.
I need to take a moment and reflect
On what you mean to me, God.
As days go by,
I will appreciate you
Search for you
And give love to you.
I hope that you will wait for me,
As you have for so long,
Until I find you.

Ara Cho, age 14
Saint Elizabeth Ann Seton Parish, Irvine, CA

Help Me Jesus

Jesus, things rarely go my way, but I'm glad that they go yours.
I try to be peaceful like you want, but life is like a war.
I don't mind the problems,
because I know you'll get me through.
I need you here to guide me and show me what to do.
I try hard to ignore the pain I feel inside.
I try to be strong, while you are my guide.
The weight upon my shoulders begins to crush my back.
As I walk toward a better life, I step on many tacks.
My sadness becomes stronger as I'm weakened by the pain.
But because I have you in my life, I am not yet slain.
I try not to argue, it's for my own good.
You've given me what I needed to survive as best as I could.
I've forced some laughs for you,
but sometimes I break down and cry.
I'm glad to feel pain for you, but can't help wondering why.
I try to live my life by the example that you gave.
You said to give love to everyone so that I can be saved.
I'm having difficulty, from rarely being treated right.
I'm only human, I can't help feeling spite.
Please help me to deny those feelings and to find ways to cope.
You know how hard I'm trying to hold on to faith and hope.
I always want my heart to be a place for God to live.
But it has become hard to carry, because all it does is give.
My love goes to many people but never comes to me.
Will you try to change that? That's no way to be.
My love might become stronger, if some of it's my own.
If I ever gain self-love, I won't feel so alone.
It always gets poured out in vain, until there's nothing left.
If this does continue, I'll end up bereft.
It isn't at all easy to do God's will.
It remains my main purpose in life that I try to fulfill.
What can I do to please God? Why did God put me here?
I don't know what I'm doing, that's why I keep you near.

You know better than anyone how I get led astray.
I'm sorry that I hurt you. I wish my sins would go away.
At times my existence becomes bleak, at times I'm at my worst.
I feel ashamed afterward, you should always come first.
Please help me to do good on earth, however long I'm here.
Whatever trouble awaits me, you help me hold back fear.
I wish I could see and feel you, I wish you wouldn't hide.
But I still love you as a best friend, knowing you're at my side.
I know I'm not worthy of your love. God didn't give me pride.
But I still wish I could embrace you
and show the love I feel inside.
Jesus, what I want most is to see things through your eyes.
Cradled in your hands, is where my soul lies.

Carla Schreiber, age 17
Our Lady of Lourdes High School, Poughkeepsie, NY

It's going to happen sometime,
though I don't know when or how.
It's going to happen sometime,
and I wish it would happen **NOW!**
Sometime in the near future
people will learn to love.
Sometime in the near future
if not here, then in heaven above.
The world would be a better place
if it would happen now.
It's going to happen sometime
though I don't know when or how.

Sarah Fons, age 13
Saint Anthony on the Lake Parish, Pewaukee, WI

Dear Lord,
Help us to put our lives in perspective, to channel our thoughts not so much on the menial things of day-to-day life but on the lessons and attitudes that will be with us throughout the duration of our time on earth. Help us to realize that the building of reputation and status is insignificant compared to the importance of building moral judgement and strong relationships with others, ourselves, and God. Help us to understand that our bodies and minds are your greatest gifts to us, and that when we love whatever you have bestowed upon us, we will consequently love what you have given others. Let us not succumb to feelings of envy, but to realize that you have great things in store for everyone. You have instilled in all of us some degree of love, compassion, and understanding. Help us to amplify and utilize these gifts when we deal with everyone—our peers, our families, our allies, and our antagonists. All in your name we pray. Amen.

Kendall Kay Krajicek, age 15
Saint Patrick Parish, Gretna, NE

My Heaven

As I lay awake
And watch the time go by,
I wonder as I shed another tear:
If only there were no hatred,
No violence, no war . . .
And all that was left was
Love and happiness . . .
Then we would be home.

Emily Catherine Nichols, age 13
Saint Peter Middle School, Joplin, MO

Dear God,
To the world from you I ask,
  A few small yet large tasks.
Love for those who have no one,
  And happiness for those who don't have fun!
Faith for those who don't believe,
  And strength for those who must grieve.
Hope for those without a king,
  And a king for those who have nothing.
Clothes for those who go bare,
  And kindness for those who don't care.
Peace for those who feel they must fight,
  And joy for those who can't see the light.
Justice for those wrongfully accused,
  And joy for those who aren't amused.
Dear God, I know there's more than a few,
  But God I only wish I could do them for you!

Amelia, age 12
Saint Joseph High School, Madison, MS

I look to you, your hands outstretched.
Protect me in your grasp.
Let the warmth that surrounds your face
Allow my hate and sin to pass.
Let me give you all my problems
And the answers on your mind,
Are to live the days so simply.
Just seek and you shall find.
Let me be thankful for the things
I have, I need, I love.
For you help me see that all these things
are better than enough.
Without you, independence
May be quite a path to take.
There's too much that I could risk
Or lots of things for me at stake.
Still, the guidance that you give
Is ever present in my day,
The reassuring feeling that
You'll never go away.
I look to you and see
All your beauty within myself,
Because loving someone like you, God,
Is like loving no one else.

Ashley Benson, age 16
Padua Academy, Wilmington, DE

Dear and Loving God,
I have known you, loved you, and believed in you my whole life.
I am not going to stop now. I can't tell you how big of a role you
play in my life.

I have been taught so much about you, but I am not sure
what to believe. I want to learn what is right, not wrong. Help

me to realize that you are always with me and all I have to do is put my faith in you and I will know what to do.

You saved us by dying on the cross. For what you did for us I am very grateful. I would just like to say thank you for always being there for me and for saving me. Amen.

Brigid Feely, age 13
Saint Thomas Aquinas School, Buffalo, NY

Love That Conquers Polluted Times

My existence remains incomplete, but no longer feels flawed.
Though your eyes told me not to lose myself, I lost myself to you.
Absorb each smile of my being;
And prepare to catch my final tears with warm hands.
Tears were painful until you let me cry.
I remained a **shadow** until you showed me
Suffering means possession of a heart.
A quiet moment found me in random existence.
You blindly saw the embittered confusion disappear
As this vagabond challenged prestige and spoke.
Silent recollection embraces me in mysterious prayer.
I know love that conquers polluted times.
I hope for no end that proves falseness.
You have that light: the look that tells me to
Take as much time as necessary to grow up.
In union with you, I feel colors, see music.
You always did treat my heart better than anyone else.
You provided me with the desire to breathe.

Andrea Wass, age 15
Academy of the Holy Cross, Kensington, MD

Sometimes I lay awake
wondering what to do.
I wait for you to give me a sign.
but nothing comes.
There is one question
I have always pondered:
Are you there for me?
I hope and I pray, so
when my problem has
been solved, I know
you have been working
where I can't see you,
down in my soul,
showing me what is right
and my path of life.

Lynse Wolfe, age 14
Vandebilt High School, Houma, LA

Thank You, God, for providing me with a home, with a
  loving family,
for giving me the greatest friends,
for helping during times when I am not my best,
for giving me the strength I need to go on,
for giving me hands and feet to do your work,
for providing me with a voice to speak about good and
a conscience that helps me decide what is right and wrong,
for giving me talent to entertain others,
for helping me to cope with those with whom I am not friends,
and for giving me a life to do good.

Carol Rose, age 13
Saint Gerard School, Paterson, NJ

Baptized in Tears

The beginnings of a prayer roll
Down my face. It traces all
The things I have to lose.
And I have so much to lose.
The prayer salves each worry
And washes away doubt,
Leaving only faces of the
Ones I love. Through blurred
Eyes, all of creation wears a halo.
The prayer baptizes my face with
The waters of the River Jordan
Flowing from my eyes.
The salty covenant floods
My mouth, and a single
Question escapes:
Why do I cry when I pray?

Sarah, age 15
Visitation Academy, Saint Louis, MO

Hello again, God. I'm in church because church always makes me feel close to you. I feel bad, God, because my mom's mad at me. I was in a really bad mood when I got home and I was kind of rude to her. I feel so sad. God, could you please forgive me? I'm going to try to never be like that again and to think before I speak because I really didn't mean it. Thank you, God. Now I'm going to find her and tell her I'm sorry. Thanks for always being forgiving.

Emily Cullings, age 12
Catholic Central High School, Troy, NY

Please, God
always be there
through good times
and in bad times.
and even in sad times.
never leave my soul,
then I'll be all alone,
without you.
I'll try
not to hurt you,
I'll really try
hard,
For I believe
in you.

Jamie Lanuez, age 11
Holy Spirit School, Pequannock, NJ

Faith

When I was young I used to dream about my future.
Now I know that I am living in that future and it is very different
    than what I imagined it would be.
It hasn't all been beautiful.
Some of it has been scary, and painful, and sad.
But through it all, I've grown and lived my life with joy, courage,
    and hope that I would make it through each day and find
    tranquility in each new one.
There have been times when my faith was not as strong as it was
    when I was small.
Yet, I know that whatever the future brings, I must always believe
    that God will guide me and care for me.

Edviemarie Clark, age 13
Saint Philip the Apostle School, Clifton, NJ

Please God, grant me length . . .
Length in time
Length in hugs,
Length in conversations,
Length in life.

Please God, grant me width . . .
Width in views,
Width in opinions,
Width in varieties,
Width in life.

Please God, grant me depth . . .
Depth in ideas,
Depth in feelings,
Depth in thoughts,
Depth in life.
Please God, as I go about my day I would like to ask you to help
me make every aspect of my life more 3-D in your love. Amen.

Annie Veys, age 17
Mercy High School, Omaha, NE

Dear God,
I know you will always listen,
I know you will always care,
I will always know that you will never give up on me,
No matter what I do.
So I'll come right out and say I love you,
And thanks for caring.
I hope that I can live a long and wonderful life.
When the time comes for me to leave earth,
I hope and pray to see you in heaven.

Laura Marie Gerson, age 12
Saint Mary Parish, Winona, MN

name

i am so thirsty for
that beyond your name.
and are you only real to the dreamers?
those half sane? those satisfied with pallid, albino truths?
what color are you?
i do not mean race.
sometimes i can see you, deeper than the depths of my spirit.
i refuse to defer it as mirage. to insult you.
i know you only as
the ocean can in her last glimpses of sunset,
the logic of her madness brimming with dying sun,
those evanescent tatters too buoyant to drown.
you are chaos falling into understanding,
joyous apex,
briefly touching shining eyes
of the dying and newborn. you smile there.
you are rampant inside questions,
stretching, indigo blue, and
seeping from the pores of all night-thoughts:
the dripping holes of midnight's plush carpeting.
you are the moon's glimmering descant.
and do you weep for me?
i'm so thirsty, my God.

Caroline Ennis, age 17
Mercy Academy, Louisville, KY

Dear Jesus,

At times when I think there is no hope, you step into my life. You
teach me wrong from right and right from wrong, but in your
own mysterious way, through other people's actions and words. I
thank you, Jesus, for giving me the beautiful things on the earth

to respect, enjoy, and appreciate. I also thank you for giving me the not-so-beautiful things to learn from. Now, Jesus, I open the doors to my heart for you. Only you have the keys to my heart. Amen.

P.S. I feel you with me as I read this softly to myself.

Brooke Barto, age 11
Sacred Heart Academy, Redlands, CA

Where's God?

In a society where perfection is life's main goal,
    where does God fit in?
When your parents are your last resource for love,
    where does God fit in?
In the only society where people starve themselves to be beautiful,
    where does God fit in?
When what's on the outside is more important than what's inside,
    where does God fit in?
When popularity is the most important thing,
    where does God fit in?
And when life can be hell, where's God?

"Here I am," says God.
"God why does all this awful stuff happen every day?"
"Say a prayer," says God.
"Okay, God."
Thank you.

Margaret Meyerhoff, age 13
Blessed Trinity Catholic Community, Orlando, FL

Distraction

God, are you there?
I finally made time for you.
So how are you, God?
Oh, hold on God, my friend needs me.
Yes, God could you hold on for her?
I'm back God. So where was I?
I wanted to tell you that . . .
Oh no, I'm sorry I can't hear you, God.
The radio's too loud. Hold on, God,
My favorite song is on.
Yes, God, hold on for this.
Anyway, what will you do for me?
Look my favorite TV show is on.
Hold on for this, God.
Yes, God, hold on for this.
I have to go now.
But I will spend time with you tomorrow.

Gina Louhisdon, age 17
Holy Family High School, Glendale, CA

Dear God,

Thank you so much for the gift of my parents. They are great.
I would like to ask for help for them though. Please help them
acquire the strength they need to go to work every day and come
home to the unending job of parenting. God, help my family to
always work out our difficulties and always have a good relationship. I know that they are not perfect, and I love them for that. I
love you too, God, and I appreciate all that you have done and
all that you can do for me. Amen.

Rebecca Ellen Wolff, age 14
Resurrection of Our Lord School, Saint Louis, MO

God, help me!
I feel like my life is not under my control. Everything is haywire. And the only thing that I think I have under control is myself. So . . .
Help me to *be happy* with who I am.
Help me to have the courage to stand up for what I believe.
Help me to have patience with my teachers, friends, and parents.
Help me to *understand* the actions and feelings of those around me.
Help me to be responsible in all the decisions I make.
Help me to trust that you, God, will protect and guide me.
Help me to *be open* to new people, ideas, and opportunities.
Help me to overcome my fears of rejection, failure, and the future.
Help me to make a positive difference in my world.
Help me to *love life* and all of its wonderful possibilities.

Rebecca Jansen, age 18
Saint Joseph Academy, Saint Louis, MO

Morning Prayer

Time,
Each second there to cherish.
I choose my fate.
I know I cannot turn back time.
Yesterday has passed.
I'm unable to change the way I've acted.
All I can do is look to the future and hope for your forgiveness.
You've given me a new day.
I want to seize each new day you give me,
With your loving intercession.
I've experienced many things before that I wouldn't have without
    your wings.
You guide me and teach me through your love.
But sometimes my heart is closed to that love.
Today my spirit can choose to radiate through the dismal clouds,
    or be a dismal cloud itself.
Help me make my day sunlight,
And let that sun shine through me in the hearts of others.
And when this day has ended, let me remember the sun and the
    rainbow, but look to the stars.
Amen.

Lindsie N. Jung, age 16
Marian Heights Academy, Ferdinand, IN

Dear God,

Sometimes I do the wrong thing or make a bad decision. Please help me to do the things I know are right and help me to realize my mistakes. Lead me to the right path and away from the wrong. Sometimes it's hard to stay away from the wrong path, especially when all of my friends take that path and encourage me to go with them. Help me to be a leader and take the path that will lead me to heaven. Make me a dancer whose feet take me the right way. Help me to hold my head high, be confident, courageous, and always smile. When a dancer moves her feet the wrong way, or makes a mistake, she keeps going, she keeps smiling, and doesn't try to cover it up. She notices her mistake and does better next time. Please give me the gift of a dancer, to keep going, to learn from my mistakes, and to do better in the future. Give me the wisdom to be a good leader in society and set good examples. Help me to perform my life like a dancer performs her routines—with courage, confidence, and leadership. Amen.

Allie Abbruzzese, age 13
Saint John the Baptist School, Silver Spring, MD

I'm joyful today,
Because a breeze is blowing,
The grass is green,
I'm God's child and God loves me!
I'm happy today,
Because a bird is singing in the tree,
I told God I'm sorry and God has forgiven me!
I'm hopeful today,
Because the sun has risen,
The sky is blue,
God has let me start anew!
I'm thankful today,
Because Jesus has died for me and you,
Thanks for loving me God, and God . . .
I love you too!

Katie Kalinowski, age 13
Saint Elizabeth Ann Seton Parish, Saint Charles, MO

Prayer of Confidence

Please read while looking into a mirror.

I dream, but fear to try.
I try, but fear to fail.
I fail, but fear to try again.
I am trapped in an unending cycle of anxiety.
To be positive about myself, my talents, and my capabilities,
That is what I dream but fear to try,
Try but fear to fail,
Fail but fear to try again.
God, save me from myself and this entrapment.
You made me in your likeness.
I am beautiful.
You gave me a mind to think for myself.
I am intelligent.
You made me different from everyone else,
I am unique.
You gave me talents and ambition.
I have desire.
God, give me the confidence to be myself,
To love who I am and what I can do,
To take all that you have given me,
And offer it all to you.

S. G., age 18
Immaculate Heart Academy, Washington Township, NJ

Millennium Poem

What if the world had come to an end,
would we all be in heaven safe again?
What if we used up all the resources needed,
would we be called genius, or just conceited?
What if we all could turn back time,
would it be an adventure, or a nightmare in our minds?
What if the world could be peaceful forever,
could we all live in happiness together?
Now that the last millennium has passed,
the question remains, will the next one last?

Bethany Perillo, age 12
Holy Spirit School, San Antonio, TX

Dear God,

Help me to help others in my daily life.
Help me to be kind to everyone I meet.
Help me to do my best in all my work.

Be with me as I make decisions in my life.
Be with me as I live each day to the fullest.
Be with me when I need you most.

Forgive me when I sin.
Forgive me when I hurt others.
Forgive me when I make wrong decisions.

But most of all, God help me to do what you would have done.
Amen.

Sarah Dalton, age 12
School of the Holy Child, Rye, NY

God,
Why are some people so selfish?
Me, me, me,
That's all they think about.
How can I get richer?
How can I be more important?
Inside,
I want to scream,
Don't you get it?
You are important!
Someone cares for you.
You are special.
You are unique.
You are somebody's joy.
Just sitting there,
scheming away
to make yourself number one.
But you forget!
There is always one,
At least one person,
Who thinks you are number one—the best.
Give up?
It's God.

Emma Lueger, age 12
Saint Robert School, Shorewood, WI

Why is the world the way it is?
Why is it full of wrong?
Why are her eyes so big?
Why is his neck so long?

Why is she so dark?
Why am I so light?
Why is she called black?
Why am I called white?

Why am I so tall?
Why are you so short?
Why is she so kind?
Why does he have no heart?

Why is there such a thing as war?
Why do people die?
Why do people cheat and steal?
Why do people lie?

Why are people so prejudiced?
Why do people judge?
Why do they point their fingers at others?
Why do they hold a grudge?

Why do people make promises,
that they know they cannot keep?
Why do people cry?
Why do they have to weep?

Why do people have to suffer?
Why do they have to be ill?
Why do some people get so much to eat,
when others don't even get a meal?

Why are there so many problems
with answers on which we cannot rely?
Why are there no explanations?
Why are there so many whys?

Jennifer Roy, age 15
Catholic High School of Pointe Coupee, New Roads, LA

I have always wondered
Why the sky is a magnificent blue,
Why the sun has such warmth,
Why the clouds look like pillows of cotton candy,
Why the stars dance in the sky,
Why the oceans can be so peaceful,
Why pets are such a comfort,
Why the flowers make a rainbow on land,
Why a sunset and sunrise are such beautiful paintings in the
   sky,
Why people are so different,
And why I was put on this earth.
But the one question that has puzzled me the most is what
God looks like. Then one day I took some advice. I stopped my
wondering and stepped back taking a look at God's creation. It
was then that I realized, we have the truest, the most beautiful
picture of God. All we have to do is look and really see!

Ellen Dohogne, age 14
All Saints School, Saint Peters, MO

Every Step and Breath
I Take You Are There

As I step onto the starting line, I begin
to tremble. I make the sign of the cross,
knowing that you'll be with me
throughout the entire race. The gun
goes off, I'm making my way to the
front. Third, second, and finally leading the
pack, with your help, God. I know I
have to keep my pace or else I will fall
back, but with you God,
there is no falling back.
Every step I take, I know that you are with me.
Every breath I take, I know that you are with me.
I pray and pray that your angels will lift
my feet up onto their wings and help my
legs fly to the finish like they've never flown before.
I finish, and again I
make the sign of the cross in thanks that
you have helped me do the best I can.
God is within me.
Amen.

Sarah Sak, age 15
West Catholic High School, Grand Rapids, MI

O God,

You are young and old but I am in the middle. So when I am too
young to do something and too old at the same time, help me to
find something for me.

Martha Josephson, age 12
Saint Robert School, Shorewood, WI

Hey, God,
I know you can hear me.
Why can't I hear you?
I know you're here,
Exactly where, I don't know.
I can't see you, but you're here.
I see you through others.
I can feel you. I know you're watching me.
But why?
I know you love me.
Why is there evil when you created good?
Why is there hatred when you created love?
How can people hate others, when we're called to love?
I know you have an answer, but I'll have to wait to find the
     answer myself.
You have a plan for everyone.
Everyone has a journey.
It's up to us to follow or not.
Help me follow, Lord. I want to, but sometimes it's hard.
People make me lose touch with my heart.
Then I lose touch with you.
Help me follow when times are hard and people make fun of
     me.
Help me, Lord!

Angela Schleeper, age 13
Saint Elizabeth/Saint Robert School, Saint Charles, MO

Love Prayer

Thank you God, for the many ways you have shown me
that I am loved.
The very fact that you brought me into your creation shows me
that I am loved.
I see your love shine through the smiles of all my friends,
and in the sun and the stars that shine bright.
I taste your love when my mom cooks me lasagna,
even when she burns it.
I hear your love when my sister says, "I miss you",
or "drive home safely."
I feel your love when my dog licks my face
and when my cat falls asleep on my lap.
I smell your love when my dad gives me birthday flowers
or when I smell the pine scent of Christmas.
God, you awaken each and every one of my senses
with your copious love.
Every morning I wake up, and every night I fall asleep,
I know I am loved by you.
And for all these things I am grateful.
Thank you, God.
I love you.

Caroline Mary Bagnall, age 18
Greensburg Central Catholic High School, Greensburg, PA

Dear God,
Like an infant sleeps peacefully in its mother's arm,
May You cradle me close to you, safe from all harm.
Like the cool, refreshing wind that blows through the trees,
May the renewing breath of your spirit set my troubled heart at
    ease.
Like sheep follow shepherds, never uncertain or afraid,
May I always trust in your care and walk in your ways.
Like the sun never fails to rise each morning in the sky,
May I as faithfully remember to give you thanks day and night.
Like a child marvels at a rainbow or a mighty crash of thunder,
In awe may I praise you for your great power and wonders.
Like a fire in the hearth gives comfort against the cold,
May the warm flame of your love be kindled in my soul.
And like raindrops pour from the sky to fall upon my face,
May you open up the heavens and shower me with your grace.
Amen.

Mary Elizabeth Klein, age 16
John F. Kennedy Catholic High School, Saint Louis, MO

Hold me like a baby
When I cannot get to sleep.
Bury me in your softness,
comfort me as I weep.
Let me lose myself in you,
every facet of your being.
Let me embrace you wholly,
and see as you are seeing.
May my sins, my hate, my guilt
melt in the furnace of your arms.
Just hold me like a baby
as in you, I am reborn.

Jessica Pharris, age 17
Mercy Academy, Louisville, KY

Time and time again
I find myself staring out the window,
Looking back on God's creation.
When a day meant the world,
And life had no meaning yet.
And I wonder,
What if God had changed one thing,
Or even two?
What if she looks back and says,
"I could have done better?"
Even so,
A day would still mean the world
And life would be an immortal venture
In a mortal world.
Time and time again
I find myself staring out the window.

Catherine Popp, age 14
Benilde-Saint Margaret School, Saint Louis Park, MN

shouts and whispers
of growing girls

As You Grow

Your time to be a little girl
won't come again.
That thought may be sad
for someone who doesn't know
how beautiful your youth
has been.
The memories of loving
and living will last forever
but now . . .
Your future as a woman
is even more exciting,
you are a masterpiece.
You go now, to bring beauty
to the world,
to be a strong woman
of great compassion.
As you step away, rejoice!
For whatever distance
comes between us,
I will share your days of sunshine
and help whisk away the clouds;
our hearts bound together
in a special love.

Hallie Wallen, age 16
Knoxville Catholic High School, Knoxville, TN

I am like a single rose,
Giving everyone a beautiful sight;
Holding my head up,
And standing **tall.**
Till my old dying days
I'll give everyone who has helped me praise
For fighting my way
Each and every day.
And some people think that I'm just
An ordinary girl
That they can try to put down.
But if they look really hard at me
They'll see that I'm going to be
The best that I can be.

Erica Brown, age 15
Archdiocese of Chicago, Chicago, IL

God Is Always There

When your best friend tells your secret and the whole sixth grade laughs, God doesn't laugh.

When the boy you like starts liking someone else that is skinnier, prettier, and a cheerleader, God still likes you.

When you have your heart set on being a cheerleader and you do not make it, God is there.

When you do not make the basketball team, God is on your team.

When everyone wears the same kind of outfit to the dance, but your mom will not get you the outfit, God doesn't care how you are dressed.

When your mom does not let you go to a friend's house, God is in your house.

I bet if God were here in the sixth grade, God would be the coolest sixth grader. Knowing God is by my side, I can make it through everything.

Susan Jean Pinkes, age 11
Saint James Parish, Corinth, MS

i look
into the mirror
and see the
shining face
of a girl
scared and
vulnerable,
that much to say
the least.
I look into those innocent
shining eyes
and realize
those eyes have seen
too much
those ears have heard
too much
that mind has known
too much
ever to be called
little.
i look into that
hallway mirror
and realize
this is not
a young girl
but the struggling
blurry reflection
of a striving
young woman.

Rebecca Jane Kreitzer, age 14
Saint Odilia School, Shoreview, MN   •

Who I Am

I look in the mirror
And I realize
That there is something
behind these eyes.

There is a child
Waiting to come out.
There is a cautious person
Full of worry and doubt.

There is a woman
With unconditional love.
There is a girl with
Faith in God above.

There are experiences from
Which I have grown.
There are friends and family
And the love that they have shown.

There is the future
And what lies ahead.
There are things to be done
And words to be said.

There are strangers
Whom I'll meet along the way.
They will be my guiding lights
From day to day.

If I had a chance to change
Who I am and will be,
I would not
Because I accept me for me.

Cassandra G. Sautter, age 13
Saint Joseph School, West Milford, NJ

Canticle of a Girl

How great is the Lord my God;
I am Molly, God's child, who will praise God
Until the end of time.
My soul dances with God,
My spirit soars.
To me, God gives great gifts;
God's love is endless like the sea.
Holy is the One who lights the darkness,
Who guides me in my time of need.
God my Savior holds me in strong arms,
And brings comfort to my weak body.
God walks with me;
Never am I alone.
God shows mercy to me, a sinner;
And frees me from all evils.
In God do I trust;
The One who knows my deepest secrets.
God leads the church with a mighty hand;
The faithful are God's humble servants.
Forever will I praise my God;
The One who saves me from my torment
And rescues me from despair.

Mary Clare Kelly, age 14
Saint Katharine of Siena School, Wayne, PA

Dancing with God

Ever since I was little, my parents have said that I will be a
dancer. When I was two and started to walk, I always walked on
my tiptoes. This was the start of my dancing career. Everyone
else started counting 1-2-3-4, but at the age of three I learned to

count 5-6-7-8 in dance. At age fifteen, I still dance and love every minute of it. God has given me a talent that at times has meant hard work and sacrifice. I know just to dance is not enough. I must dance from the heart and believe in myself as God believes in me. Before I go on stage, I mentally go through my routine. I think about not being alone on stage. I feel that God is dancing with me, embracing me. It is very easy to relax, smile, and dance in the arms of your Maker. I go on stage feeling relaxed and knowing the great, loving God is with me. God simply whispers, "Trust me," and the performance begins as if in a dream. "Commit everything you do to the Lord. Trust God, and God will help you" (Psalm 37:5).

Amanda Papania, age 15
Mother of Mercy High School, Cincinnati, OH

Thanks for crying! Thanks for that simple act of crying when I told you something sad, scary, and shocking but true. That secret was locked up inside me, like a prisoner waiting to be set free. You gave me that freedom, and now, I don't think as much about the secret as I did before. So thanks, my dear, precious friend! I wouldn't know what to do without you, and I know you think so too. I'd be lost without you in my life, at school and in my home life. The **ups**, the **downs**, and as a friend, I'll truly thank you until the end. I'm trying to say thanks—not only for being the sensational friend to me that you are, but most importantly thanks for being there for me. If it weren't for you to tell my deepest darkest secret to, I may not be here today.

Kristina M. Murray, age 13
Saint Gabriel the Archangel Parish, Neenah, WI

I am an in-betweener.
Far from the so-called dorks,
Yet, far from ever being popular.
It'll always be this way,
Because I'm an in-betweener.

I am an in-betweener.
No boy would ever go out with me.
But they are my friends.
Doesn't matter that in the long run it won't matter.
It'll always be this way,
Because I'm an in-betweener.

I am an in-betweener.
I'm never the best on any team,
Yet I get the satisfaction of saying I'm on the better one.
No matter what my mom can say,
It'll always be this way,
Because I'm an in-betweener.

E. Radzwion, age 13
Jackson Catholic Middle School, Jackson, MI

I am a horse galloping free in the wind.
Nothing can catch me,
I am going too fast.
Running away from the violence in the world
And the pollution that makes the world a mess.
I run to places I have never been,
To explore and adventure and think
And dream.

Claire T. Pacha, age 13
John F. Kennedy Catholic School, Davenport, IA

felicity (fe lis' i ti)   *1. Happiness, that which causes happiness.*
2. Gracefulness of expression, an apt and graceful remark.

When I heard my time was running out

I reached up like you said.
I stopped so fast my mind went blank
Thought leaked out of my head.
And I slowed down.
Now I've learned how to dance, feeling weightless and free,
Unchained in the sea of the sky.
And I've flown like the phoenix rising out of the ash
Leaving heads turned wondering why.
I slowed down.
I traded in my wristwatch for a pair of jade bracelets
Trying to soothe my mental state.
The lengths I can go to escape my confines
In order to be something that can't wait.
'Cause it's the Philistines who have no time.
And I'd rather dance with the angels
Than hang up my halo in the locker room,
Sitting in the closet writing poems that shouldn't rhyme.

Laura Jablonski, age 17
Stella Maris High School, Rockaway Park, NY

My Life as a Girl

From the start of being a girl I would never really think of why I was really put on the earth. To me it was always just about clothes, dolls, and makeup, the most important things I would ever use. To me, weekends were for going to the mall, not to church. I wouldn't have thought about going to church, even if I had time. I realized that there was a church in my town when my parents decided that it was time to become a part of this celebration. To me now, a girl's life is not just about clothes, dolls, and makeup; its about life and a connection with God.

Victoria Lincoln, age 11
Christ the King School, Rutland, VT

In a far-off place, I hear the sound of a blaring beep that never stops, then I realize it is my alarm and I slam it hard enough to hurt my hand and wake me up. I eventually get up and take my shower. I go through the whole routine of getting ready for school, making sure I look good to go to an all-girl school, but I do it all for impression. I almost liked it when I was a very unpopular sophomore and didn't have to look good. I went to school just to learn but got made fun of the whole day and was the loneliest person in the school.

God . . .
Why is it that I have to try so hard to have friends?
Why do I have to be the best to have companionship?
These are questions I will never have an answer to, but guide me
through prayer to help me understand.

Kristen Holly Shadburn, age 16
Holy Family High School, Glendale, CA

Look at Me

When I look at me and see
what I've come to be
I thank God for all he has done
For me. I try to look
at myself as a young black child
striving to be happy and proud.
I try not to look at myself as
an unwanted child in a gang with
the wrong crowd. I try to look at
myself as a college student,
going to school every day and
thanking God every step of the way.
I try not to look at myself as the
unknown and a nobody. I try to
look at myself as a nice person who
does the right thing. I try not
to look at myself as a mean person
going around and keeping all
that anger inside. Most of all
I try to look at myself ten
years from now, thinking I am
going to be happy.
Why and how?

Kamela Hamilton, age 14
Archdiocese of Chicago, Chicago, IL

Dear God,
Growing up is hard sometimes. Other girls may feel alone and not know what to do. They think that they have nobody to turn to. God, when I feel that way, I think of you. You have sent me three large gifts in my life. I think of them as miracles. You have given me my best friends. I don't know what I would do if I had never met them. We were brought to each other. We get along easily and always have fun. Although that's only part of why they're important to me. I don't feel uneasy around them, and they're always there to listen to me and give me as much self-confidence as they can give. Lord, I thank you every day of my life for blessing me with friends that I know will always be there for me. Amen.

Jessie Leigh Coop, age 13
Venerini Academy, Worcester, MA

I Am Her

I saw an angel just like me
Running in the wild, letting it be.
She was beautiful, free, great, and clean.
She had smooth flowing hair and big, gentle eyes.
She looked happy, gorgeous, and wise.
All of a sudden it started to rain.
She gradually disappeared,
Losing her character.
And I saw she was no other
Than my own reflection.
As I started to remember
I'm a child of God
Beauty is looking beyond the skin.

Alexx, age 15
Holy Family High School, Glendale, CA

Please Help Me to Be Myself

As I am growing up I see,
So many things a girl should be.
  We should be paper thin,
  We must have the clearest skin.
  We must look like a perfect model.
  We must have that hair color,
  Even if it is out of a bottle.
  We must have the most fashionable clothes,
  And the coolest car if we drove.
  We must have the best hairstyle,
  Even though we know it will change in a while.

All these things a girl is supposed to be,
When all I really want to be is me.
  I don't need to be paper thin,
  Or have the clearest skin.
  I don't want to look like a skinny model,
  Rather a healthy sports player.
  I don't want that bottled color hair,
  I would rather have people stare at my natural hair.
  I don't want the fashionable clothes that will make me moan
      and groan,
  I would rather wear something I could bear to stay in.
  And when I drive I don't want the coolest car,
  Just one that will let me go far.
  I don't want the best hairstyle,
  Because I know that it will change in a while.
  I would rather have a hairstyle, that I would want to live with
      for a while.
All these things we are pressured to be.
So please, dear God, help me to realize
That to be just like YOU,
Is the coolest thing that I could ever do. Amen.

Amanda Marie Magnan, age 14
Saint Raphael School, Saint Louis, MO

Dance

God has granted me a splendid gift
filled with laughter, pain, and joy.
Bestowed upon me was this splendid talent,
Expressing emotion through my movements;
To laugh, cry, and sing through choreography.
Ouch!
Ah!
Yes!
No!
Errrr!
Finally!

Twirl
Run
Leap
Spin
Crash
Embrace

Discipline is strict,
Schedules are rigorous,
Performing is exhilarating,
The dance is captivating.

Expression without words,
Anger without violence,
Hurt without tears,
Love without heartbreak.

It is a passion,
It is a connection
Between people who feel emotion,
And its emotion can be shared.

Movement is a language
Spoken through feelings,
Spoken through steps and actions.

A smile
A reach
A wink
A stretch

Allowing the mute to have a voice,
The deaf to have sound,
The numb to have feeling.

I have!
I desire!
I share!
I dance!

Juliana Tyson, age 15
Marymount High School, Los Angeles, CA

Dear God, change is a big part of life.
Many things are rapidly changing in our lives right now
    and we struggle to adapt.
So we pray to you, dear Lord,
    to help us to overcome the abrupt, oncoming obstacles in life.
We pray that you will enable us,
    with the wisdom of the Holy Spirit,
    to make the best decisions in life,
    regardless of how big or small they may be.
We want to reach out and help others;
    yet at the same time, we yearn to be helped as well.
Help us to be fully aware of what's happening in our lives.
We thank you, Lord, for the gift of life
    and the strength and support you give us to face each day.

Grace Krupa, age 14
Padua Academy, Wilmington, DE

God Knows

When you are tired and discouraged from fruitless efforts,
God knows how hard you have tried.
When you've cried so long and your heart is in anguish,
God has counted your tears.
If you feel that your life is on hold and time has passed you by,
God is waiting with you.
When you're lonely and your friends are too busy even for a
phone call,
God is by your side.
When nothing makes sense and you are confused or frustrated,
God has the answer.
If suddenly your outlook is brighter and you find traces of hope,
God has whispered to you.
When things are going well and you have much to be thankful
for,
God has blessed you.
Remember that wherever you are or whatever you are facing,
God knows!

Yee Yan Lai, age 17
Marian Heights Academy, Ferdinand, IN

I thought I had been doing all right lately, but Mom has
been more and more upset with me. Sometimes it's just so hard
to stay afloat. I felt myself drowning—spiraling lower and lower.
Finally I couldn't take all the weight and I just collapsed with
one big sob. I knew that the stream of accusations coming at me
weren't true, but I felt so low I could not say anything back. I
thought of what G. L. told me, to imagine Jesus with open arms
like he's about to give me a hug.

Mom and I said very little for a while after that, until she told me to make some tea for myself and go do my homework. I started to cry again as I made the tea, but she came over and gave me a hug. For once, I didn't push her away, and I didn't let go.

Elizabeth Martin, age 18
Trinity High School, Camp Hill, PA

Carpe Diem

Take the time to smell the flowers,
For life is only made up of so many hours.
Don't be afraid to burst out with sudden laughter and joy.
Never shy away from talking to a boy.
Don't be embarrassed to burst into tears.
It is very important to face your fears.
Ride the roller coaster another time or two.
Talk to your elders or you may never discover
what they knew.
Never hesitate to say, "I love you!"
Stand up and speak your mind!
To those who are mean, be kind.
Pass out hugs for no particular reason.
Enjoy every season
As it only occurs once every year.
Don't spend too much time in front of the mirror.
Most importantly, seize the day!
or Carpe Diem! as they would say.

Andria Baker, age 18
Mercy High School, Omaha, NE

Remembrance

When I am old and gray
with wrinkles spreading
from the corners of my
faded blue eyes,
I will think about
how I came to be
myself.
I will remember
all the struggles I faced.
I will think
about things I accomplished,
the people I met,
the lives I changed.
And then . . .
I will smile.

Anna M. Bruty, age 13
John F. Kennedy Catholic School, Davenport, IA

Solitude

It was a Sunday afternoon; the weather was chilly and damp. I
had finally finished a stressful week of classes and was preparing
for the upcoming school day. My little brother was pestering
me to study with him, and I was fighting with my mother. I was
drained. I could not be rejuvenated with a healthy serving of ice
cream or by a quick power nap. I needed some time alone.

Solitude is something I cherish and anticipate. I consider it
a luxury. Most often, when I am looking to escape, I head for
my closet. It is a quiet sanctuary. On this day, I tried my usual
routine. I dragged a blanket into my closet, closed the door, and
began my quest for relaxation. However, I remained uneasy.

Consequently, I left my closet and my room and my house. I went running.

I ran the rarely traveled equestrian trail in my neighborhood. The ground remained wet from a midmorning shower, and my feet grew soggy and cold. I had forgotten gloves, and my hands were slightly numbed. Despite the conditions, I was enjoying my isolation. I felt untouchable, as though on my own tiny planet. On such a dreary day, I recognized the beauty of nature. I thought the earth was in a colorless resting period, and the gray sky was its fluffy pillow. I looked down at the ground and saw green grass poking through snow patches. I told myself that I too needed to grow and overcome obstacles like the grass. I was comparing myself to the earth. Please pardon the cliché, but I felt one with nature.

I do not know how long or how far I ran that day. I ran long enough to sort out my emotions. I recall pondering my valuable relationships with my mother and my brother. I thought about school and my priorities. Most importantly, I simply thought about my life and myself. The time I spent alone is priceless; it is truly a unique experience, a refreshing experience.

When I came home, I apologized to my mother and she, also having calmed down, returned the apology. Then I reviewed my brother's science chapter with him. Ironically, it was entitled, "Plant Growth and Responses." I silently giggled. Within the next several days, I realized how my jog had benefited me and have thus continued to run as an outlet of stress, when I need to organize my thoughts, or when I yearn for seclusion. While I run, the distractions of the world disappear and I am at peace.

Kaitlin L. Klingensmith, age 16
Greensburg Central Catholic High School, Greensburg, PA

Change

For so many years I longed to fit in.
My longing was so strong, it made my head spin.
And so, I transformed into a regular kid.
I was like everyone else in all I said and did.
How great a feeling to be part of the crowd.
My voice changed from soft to obnoxious and loud.
My hair from light brown to shocking red.
I was so cool, or so everyone said.
But beneath my red wig, I wasn't there;
My real self had vanished into thin air.
For I became the crowd
and the crowd became me.
I wonder if popularity was worth my soul.
My soul was once light, now it's black as coal.
Oh, how I wish I had not given in
And kept who I was underneath my fair skin.

Christina Corea, age 16
Corpus Christi Parish, Chatham, NJ

Dear God,

Why do we as teenagers only think about ourselves and the things that are happening around us at the present moment? Why do we worry so much about our looks and popularity? Why are we so self-conscious? so self-centered? Why do we care so much about what others think of us? Why aren't we happy with the natural beauty you gave us? Dear God, help us to be ourselves, to be all that you created us to be. Help us remember that you love us no matter what we look like. Help us to realize that everyone is popular in heaven. Thanks for listening. Amen.

Angela Marie Elgueda, age 14
Saint Patrick Parish, Corpus Christi, TX

Playing piano is one of my passions. I take pleasure in making up my own songs along the way, and love just letting the music flow. However, during my busy schedule, it gets harder and harder to sit down on the piano bench. Sometimes I find my life so busy that I can't think straight, and I ask God to help me figure things out. Often times, after praying, I find myself at the piano and begin to play. The music spools from my fingertips and the melodies I create help soothe me and clear my mind. It is nice to think that God inspired me to sit and play such beautiful things. The harmony God can create is astonishing, and I am thankful every day for that.

Lindsay, age 16
Saint Peter Parish, Geneva, IL

Puzzle Pieces

As I think about my life,
I turn and ponder my stupidity—
The numerous times
I've put my reputation in jeopardy
Just to fit in.
The times
When I've gone against the rules,
Just to appear not afraid,
Just to appear someone I am not.
I feel like a piece in a puzzle—
The puzzle of humanity.
But yet I fit nowhere.
Maybe if I act like myself,
I'll find my place in the puzzle.

Amanda M. Torres, age 14
Mount Mercy Academy, Buffalo, NY

I will catch my fireflies during the day.
I will let them go at night.

I will catch sunlight with my smile.
I will tan the hearts of others with my ultraviolet grin.

I will earn my daily bread.
I will share a slice with anyone who needs it.

I will dream more during the day.
I will sleep more at night.

I will eat more fruits and vegetables.
I will treat myself to chocolate at least once a day.

I will pick my battles.
I will not back down from the battles I chose.

I will accept my imperfections and my weaknesses.
I will share my talents and my strengths.

I will make mistakes.
I will grow from them.

I will hold my tongue.
I will open my eyes and lend an ear.

I will pay more attention to my little brother.
I will pay less attention to my television set.

I will value individual persons more.
I will value my individual schedule less.

I will say please and thank you.
I will hold the door for the people behind me.

I will sort my laundry every Friday before I go out,
because my mom wants me to.
I will read every play written by William Shakespeare someday,
because I want to.

I will leave cookies out for Santa every Christmas Eve.
I will wear a costume every Halloween.
I will not forget what it was like to be five.
I will try to understand what it is like to be fifty-five.
I will wish on stars.
I will stop to look at the sunset.

I will remember what a summer breeze feels like,
so I can recall it in January.
I will record the taste of snowflakes on my tongue,
so I can taste them in June.

I will stop to hear a crack of thunder.
I will stop to hear the pitter-patter of rain on my roof, because
you never know which will be your last.

I, Alaina Ann Farabaugh, will try to live my life
according to these standards I have set.

I will fail and I will succeed.
But more than anything else, I will try.

Alaina Farabaugh, age 15
Our Lady of Peace Parish, Erie, PA

Simple Gifts

Day passes quickly and soon night falls
The moon emanating a silvery light
Stars burning
I hear crickets singing their song;
They sing of your glory.
I soon feel sleepy and drift off to bed.
Before I sleep I look into the mirror;
I see myself and wonder.
It comes to me like a dream
I am a gift from God.
I am God's best work because I am me and I am beautiful.
I lie down.
I finally understand
We are all gifts from God.
As crickets sing their songs
So do we;
We may not sing a melody
Or carry a tune, but our hearts sing the greatest song of all
The song of compassion
Love
Hope
Kindness
Faithfulness
As a child of God, I understand
We are all gifts from God,
We are all beautiful in our own special ways.

Kelli Peters, age 11
Saint Robert School, Shorewood, WI

What is freedom?

Is it not being owned?
NO!
Freedom is a bird to fly,
Swoop,
And sing.
There is no net to catch a thing of freedom.
Freedom is a river,
Too swift and strong to catch.
Freedom is the fire in my heart
That makes me strong.
No one has the will
To put out that fire,
Except God and me.
Our mind is free to explore, anywhere.
The sky is not the limit,
As people say.
You create the limit.
Freedom is me.
Freedom is my mind, heart, soul, and me.
No one can rule me, and capture me.
I am free.

Kayla Ann Olszowy, age 11
Sacred Heart Parish, Valley Park, MO

my soul
my soul is wide open
ready for everyone to meet.
my soul is not a hollow empty tree;
it is a bird's nest full of life and ready to be explored.
I am not a little school girl;
I am a wild child,
ready to run and run until there is no more path to follow.
people say curiosity killed the cat but it hasn't killed
me yet
(hee hee)
the caffeine rushing to my head like a subway going to the
station
Katharine, why are you hanging on the wall?
my mother sometimes asks.
I am not a monkey,
I only look and act like them;
my soul can not be summed up by one or two words,
because
I'm different
unique and original,
the only one of my kind.

Katharine A. Murphy, age 13
John F. Kennedy Catholic School, Davenport, IA

Words of Caution

Be aware of
Living in a womb
Lying about loving
Manipulating too.

Be aware of
Too much freedom
And false reasoning
Having friends for only benefit
Leaving hearts weeping.

Be aware of
Sorrowful tranquility
A play on sympathy
Of figments of disasters
And lost reality.

Be aware of
Vulnerability
Brainwashed without a dream
Of leaving warmth, and backfired schemes
This black hole is deepening.
Realize things aren't always what they seem.

Jessica Hendershot, age 18
Saint Joseph Academy, Saint Augustine, FL

Seventeen Years of Knowledge

I realize life offers an orchard of laughter
despite my river of tears.
I have felt the wonder of new life and the harsh reality of death.
I know my life is molded by love and declares war on hate.
I understand when my prayers are answered
and gradually become thankful for those that are not.
I have established tremendous faith that consistently weathers a
storm of uncertainties.
I am in desperate pursuit of real truth
and try not to believe it is hard to find today.
I despise the agony of defeat and live for the glory of victory.
I am wary of excitement because disappointment may follow.
I hope for the future even though I so profoundly fear it.
I have endlessly tried and believe I will conquer despair.
I still need a hand to hold sometimes
and delight when I must be the guiding hand.
I know my words are powerful,
and yet they cannot capture the majesty of my experience.
And all of this knowledge I have acquired in just seventeen years.

Sarah Mullen, age 18
Saint Joseph Academy, Saint Louis, MO

My God is a very special person. God helps me through the
hard times and is there to watch the good times. My God touches my life every day and is there for me. God is there for you
too; just believe and God will be there for you always. My God
makes sure I'm safe and watches over me at night and wakes me
with the morning light.

God always gives us another chance. God doesn't care if you
mess up and will still love you if you do. God made you special

and you are beautiful. Don't let anyone tell you different. God loves you the way you are. When boys make fun of you, ignore them. They probably feel horrible and jealous about themselves. The most important thing I can tell you is to believe in God.

Molly Rose Schuette, age 13
Saint Pius X School, Edgewood, KY

God,
Make us a pathway.
Tell us we are beautiful and let us believe
What you tell us.

Grow us seeds
Of wisdom, love, knowledge,
Passion for life,
And compassion for those who suffer.

Let us know
When we hurt others by gossip or gestures
That can damage the soul.

God hold us;
Hold our hands
And never let go.

'Cause we love you
And need your guidance
So we may never fall,
But blossom
In everything we do. Amen.

Olivia Fadul, age 15
Holy Spirit Parish, Huntsville, AL

Back in the day,
My grandfather would read me a tale of Jonah and the whale.
I would say, "What a fishy story!"
I was only six; I couldn't see God's glory.

Back in the day,
My mother would say remember God's will.
I would nod to get her silence.
I was only eight; I forgot it still.

Back in the day,
My dad would say kneel in church, fall to your knees.
I would gripe and bow my head.
I was only ten; who was I supposed to please?

Back in the day,
My grandma would say, "For Heaven's sake, pick up your things!"
I would mumble, but still do her will.
I was only twelve; how did I know whose will to fulfill?

Now in the day,
My sponsor says, "Sugar, please sit still."
This time around I listen and do.
I'm only fourteen, and now I try to do God's will.
Now I fully understand there is higher force than me,
Something bigger than what I am and will be
Maybe through all the years, I was listening.

Claire Chicoineau, age 14
Saint Gerard Majella School, Kirkwood, MO

I am love and fear.
I have inherited my angelic wings from God.
I am built strong like a brick wall.
I was gathered by the heavens into femininity and was given to
    my mother to inherit me.
I am as precious as any man that walked the face of the earth.
I was gathered by the heavens with femininity blessed by God.
I have the right to walk the face of this earth.
Who am I? A brick wall, a brick wall.
I am as precious as any man that walked the face of this earth.
I am femininity gathered by the heavens and blessed by God.
This inheritance I plan on passing on.
The heavens are passed on to me.
I am a brick wall built with God's love which inspires me to live.
I am fear and love inspired to live in God's world.
I am a brick wall who prays to the heavens to bless me.
God, give me light to know the truth of the Way.

Titilayo Tae Kazeem
Bishop Loughlin Memorial High School, Brooklyn, NY

You have always been there.
You are a friend that I can always run to for help.
As a young girl turning into a woman
I make mistakes,
And don't know who to go to for help.
But no matter who cares about me
And wants to help—you are the One.
God.

Vita Antonina Pace, age 12
Saint Blase Catholic Community, Sterling Heights, MI

Dear God,
My life is very busy right now. I am trying to get ready for high school, and I have to make a lot of decisions. This is when I need you the most, but sometimes I forget that you are even there. Help me to remember that you are there and that you will help me. When I feel like no one cares and that my life has no purpose, help me to remember that everyone has a purpose in life. Thank you, God. Amen.

Ashley Power, age 13
Annunciation School, Webster Groves, MO

The moonlight floods down through the window, illuminating the white desk with a pale white light. My eyes adjust to the darkness and everything looks anew. My head lies relaxed and alert on my pillow. "What am I to do?" I ask, the confusion of the outside world still fresh in my mind. I take deep breaths; the confusion and the need to rush subside.

Spell out for the universe your situation. By explaining it honestly to God, you explain it honestly to yourself. The existence of fears, jealousy, and love, which I deny to myself, is acknowledged. I now understand myself better. God does not control this knowledge; it is always there for me to discover. God helps me to be honest with myself through my need to be honest with God.

Now every aspect of my situation, from my perspective, is laid out. It is as if God is holding a large board and all the puzzle pieces are tacked up. God steps back with me to look at the whole picture.

No booming voice shatters the silence with God's mandate. The moonlight still streams through the window, the flame still burns tall and bright. Instead, there is only the sound of my voice, in my mind. God and I stand together and start moving the little papers around. God suggests. I disagree; I want to try something else. I suggest. God disagrees. Between God and me the plan is decided. It is my voice that I hear, but I know it is God speaking.

The moonlight shines in the window, the flame dances on the wick. My head lies relaxed and alert on the pillow. God and I work side by side. We exchange. I learn about God and God learns about me. But most importantly, God helps me learn about myself.

Sarah Grapentine, age 17
Immaculate Heart Academy, Washington Township, NJ

God is with her.
God works for her.
God fills her.
God chooses her.
God accepts her.
God praises her.
God listens to her.
God cries with her.
God knows her.
God loves her.

We are her.

Nadia Olker, age 16
Divine Savior Holy Angels High School, Milwaukee, WI

A Prayer for Teenage Girls

All people were made in God's image.
God is our loving creator and
Cares deeply about each masterpiece.
God, let those who doubt themselves,
Especially teenage girls, see your greatness
And how lucky they are to share in your life.
Lord, let them see their own unique qualities
And help them to appreciate the work
That you have put into each one of them.
Teenage girls have so much going in their lives,
They need an extra sense of security,
That you, O God, provide willingly.
God, we realize that you are a skillful artist
Who only produces works of great quality.
Let us accept ourselves as we are, so we can follow in your way
And truly find happiness.
God, we see what you have done
And we praise your name.

Janine Accardi, age 16
Mary Louis Academy, Jamaica, NY

Index